Questions
Children
Ask

& How to Answer Them

DR. MIRIAM STOPPARD

Questions Children Ask

& How to Answer Them

A DORLING KINDERSLEY BOOK

*For Ol, Barney, Will, Ed, Oona,
Slater and Tiberio*

Dorling  Kindersley

LONDON, NEW YORK, MUNICH
MELBOURNE, DELHI

ILLUSTRATED BY CAROLINE EWEN

Managing Editor
Jemima Dunne

Managing Art Editor
Phil Gilderdale

Project Editor
Nicky Adamson

Senior Art Editor
Karen Ward

Designers
Luke Herriott
Maria Wheatley

Production
Antony Heller

Photography
Steve Gorton

First published in Great Britain in 1997 by
Dorling Kindersley Limited, 80 Strand, London WC2 ORL
A Penguin Company

Reprinted in 1997, 2001, 2002

A CIP catalogue record for this book is available from the
British Library

ISBN 978-0-7513-3333-6

Reproduced in Hong Kong by Bright Arts
Printed and bound in China by Hung Hing

See our complete product line at
www.dk.com

CONTENTS

"How does the baby get out?"

"What happens when you die?"

"Do I have to call him Daddy?"

"Why isn't my skin brown?"

"What does violence mean?"

INTRODUCTION

Writing this book has been prompted by many things, the first being my belief that children must be told the truth. This is the parents' dilemma: when facing a sensitive question, you may wish to give a truthful response but feel that your children aren't ready for the details. You'd be right on both counts; but instead of copping out, or giving a sanitized version, you can opt to provide the amount of truth your child can deal with. Children are naturally curious. From the moment they can formulate questions – at about two years of age – they will continue to bombard their parents with "Why?", "What?", "Where?" and "How?" But it is one thing to find an answer to "How do cars work?" It is quite another if the question is, "Where did I come from?" Telling the truth means starting with simple facts, and building in more complex information as your child grows up. For instance, few children can cope with the mechanics of sex before the age of eight; some will be much older before they're ready, a few younger. It's confusing to burden your child with sophisticated explanations when simpler ones would satisfy. When a child is mentally and emotionally ready for information, it's never embarrassing to give it. Your child desperately wants to learn, and is eager for clarifications of mystery and confusion. To respond to a child so concentrated should dispel most parents' diffidence, so timing is crucial.

DEVELOPING MUTUAL TRUST

Many parents believe that in tackling the facts of life, the genders must be segregated so Dad handles the boys and Mum the girls. This seems the natural order of things, but it carries little conviction if one parent is easy-going and the other is uptight. If you put yourself in your child's position, it's clearly best that the parent who is comfortable answering children's questions should shoulder the responsibility regardless of gender. To me, keeping the channels of communication open throughout childhood

and into adolescence is one of the most important roles of parents, and it is parents who must make the effort, not children. Who else would you want your children to turn to when they need information, help, advice and counsel? Yet parents continue to be flabbergasted when, as teenagers, their children become introspective, uncommunicative and dismissive. While some adolescent mood changes are inevitable, children whose early questions have been ignored or deflected are more likely to cut themselves off from their parents when really difficult questions arise.

ENCOURAGING A HEALTHY DIALOGUE

Parents whose responses are shifty or furtive when faced with controversial questions not only make it difficult to raise subjects like race, sex, religion or drugs within the family but worse, encourage their children to be furtive themselves. Parents who are open, responsive and frank encourage self-esteem, balance and fairness in their children and give them the space to think, weigh up options, decide and act responsibly. This healthy dialogue between parents and children has to begin early – from the very first question – and should continue throughout the time they are at home. That is why the answers I suggest start at the earliest age a child may begin asking questions. You are your children's first educators, and all their learning – including sex education – starts at home. Parents find themselves wondering if information, especially about sex or drugs, can harm their children, and hold back for fear that giving facts could encourage them to experiment. Nothing could be further from the truth. It's children who don't have information who explore and experiment dangerously. Contrary to what many people fear, children who have been given information about sex are not prurient, don't focus on sex or embark on early experimentation, but keep it in perspective as a normal part of life. There is plenty of research to show that good sex education does not encourage irresponsible behaviour; in fact, it does the exact opposite. Parents make it impossible for a child to act responsibly if they withhold information; this applies equally to other subjects which are generally seen as controversial, such as drugs, alcohol and smoking, or issues of potential prejudice, such as racial or religious differences.

THE RIGHT ANSWER FOR YOUR CHILD'S AGE

No one, however, can assume that being frank and honest is always easy. There are undoubtedly going to be difficult moments when words are hard to find and explanations are fugitive. That is why I felt it would be worth writing this book: not to supply advice by rote but to give a framework on which you can build your own answers as your child's understanding expands. I have given answers that are suitable for four age bands: ages 2–4, 4–6, 6–8 and 8–11. But none of these bands is definitive. Children advance and learn at different rates, so look on the bands as a guide – depending on the subject, a very bright girl of three-and-a-half might understand the answers in band 4–6, while a socially immature boy of nine might be better served by the answers in the band for 6–8 year olds. I've also written my answers so that they are suitable for both boys and girls, and to emphasize this I have alternated the sex of the child being referred to in my background information question by question, except where for obvious reasons the topics are specifically aimed at girls or boys.

As you read the answers to big questions like, "Where did I come from?" (see page 12), you'll see that the answers for successive age bands become more detailed and complex. If an older child asks a question for the first time, or an alternative version of it, you can give all the preceding information, as well as what's in the answer for your child's own age band. The aim is to choose what you need from the different bands to help you provide clear answers within what you judge to be the scope of your child's understanding, depending on age and maturity.

PREPARING YOUR ANSWERS

It would be wise, I think, for all but the most self-possessed parent to read over all the background information presented on the topic, including the cross-references. Not that you need to give it all in your answers, but it may enable you to answer more confidently if you understand the possible motivation behind your child's line of questioning. This is particularly important for issues of child protection, where you may need to recognize the danger signals behind your child's inquiries. Equally, it could help you to defuse challenging questions from children who may have picked up half-truths in the playground. It may even enable you to be clearer in your own mind on some subjects if you read the text before formulating an answer for your child. This book is also designed for sharing with your child. It is illustrated with cartoons, diagrams and pictures that you can look at together, in very much the same close way you might pick over a bedtime story or school exercise book. So the book is at one and the same time for parents to read alone and for children and parents to read together, making it easier, I hope, for you and your family to navigate a comfortable route together through even the trickiest questions.

To no child is my whole answer necessary. Pick and choose; discard and invent; reject and create. Use examples that are well-known to your family in constructing answers; for instance, when describing a certain length of time to a young child, relate it to the time between family events such as birthdays and holidays. Lard your answers with what you felt and did when you were a child, and you will become more approachable, understanding and sympathetic in their eyes.

A FOUNDATION FOR THE FUTURE

Try to see answering each of your child's questions as an opportunity to teach – not in any formal way, but the kind of teaching that every parent can pass on to a child well before they go to school: the lessons of kindness, tolerance, justice and generosity. We can socialize our children when they're very young – instilling in them everything from table manners to sexual awareness and moral values. Children have in place a clear understanding of these values (or their opposites) long before they reach the age of five, which means that you as parents are your child's most important teacher and friend – and always will be if you start off right. These are roles and responsibilities you can't refuse. And of course all the effort is worth it because what comes back is trust, respect and love. I know of few other ways of earning these precious gifts from our children. Every time you look your children straight in the eye, speak with sincerity and give an honest answer, you bond with them, and those bonds can be life-long.

QUESTIONS ABOUT

What's puberty?

Can men have babies?

How does the baby get in there?

Why have I got a penis?

What is a period?

How are babies made?

How can you tell if someone is gay?

SEX & BIRTH

All children are curious about themselves and where they came from. At the same time, they have become aware of their own bodies from infancy and soon register the difference between the sexes. As they grow older, it becomes increasingly difficult to shield them from sexual ideas in

What's a womb?

the media, and the result of all this is that they will inevitably ask questions about sex. Like many parents, you may dread these questions arising, but try not to duck the issue because you are embarrassed. Sex may have been a "no-go" topic in your family, but your young children haven't been programmed as you were. Their interest is innocent, arising out of their natural curiosity and a desire to learn, and answering their questions honestly and sympathetically is a way of loving and respecting them. Use the answers here to help you to respond to questions about sex truthfully, but in a way that is appropriate to your particular child's age and maturity, bearing in mind that few children below the age of eight can understand the

mechanics of sex. Always try to include love, emotions, feelings and values in any discussion that involves sex; combined with honesty and openness, these will help your children to go on to develop self-control and judgment about their own personal sexual behaviour when they are older.

Why was I born?

Q Where did I come from?

● *How are babies made?* ● *Why was I born?*

● *Did a stork bring me/Was I found in a cabbage patch?*

● *What is pregnant?* ● *How does the baby get in there?*

This is frequently the first question a small child ever asks about the facts of life. In an older child, it's a sign that he's beginning to have some understanding of his uniqueness as a person, but after the age of six the question may rapidly be superseded by the more knowing, "What is sex?"

WHAT'S BEHIND THIS QUESTION

The world of a young child is very self-centred and a simple answer will satisfy his curiosity. Questions often arise when you tell your child that you are expecting another baby, and this is a crucial time to be ready to answer questions about sex, reproduction and the development of a pregnancy.

If you aren't pregnant, but an older child begins to ask questions like these, it may be because he has seen something about babies at school, on TV or in a newspaper. Children over the age of six are genuinely interested in these quite profound questions.

GUIDELINES FOR YOUR ANSWERS

● Don't shrink from telling your child the truth. You owe your child an honest and open answer without any fear of being embarrassed.

● Don't feel you have to give every single detail to a young child: it's neither necessary nor good for your child, who may be frightened by what he can't grasp. It is only after about the age of eight that most children can understand the complicated mechanics of sex.

● To be sure you are answering your child's question, check it by paraphrasing: "Do you want to know how you were made when you were a baby?"

● Don't over-complicate: your six-year-old may pose the question and you find yourself embarking on a long, detailed answer, after which your child says, "No. John said he was from Newcastle; where am I from?"

WHAT ELSE TO KNOW

● With increasing age your child needs answers of increasing complexity, but without extraneous detail. Try to use words your child already understands so no further explanation is necessary.

● Remember that children are very literal. If you talk about planting a seed, they will ask you how you water it and what colour the flower will be!

● Although very young children usually accept simple explanations at face value, children over five or six often react with a "Yuk!" on first hearing about anything sexual. This is a clear sign that they can't take any more detail and in fact it is very healthy, so change the subject and try another approach next time.

Other things you may be asked...

■ *Are all babies made like that?*

■ *What's Mummy's egg/Daddy's seed?*

■ *Do Daddies make boys and Mummies make girls?*

■ *Can men have babies?*

See also *What is sex? p. 18* ● *What's a vagina? p. 20* ● *What's a penis? p. 22*

FOR AGES 2-4

A You were made in your Mummy's tummy and you grew in there safely until it was time for you to be born.

FOR AGES 4-6

A You weren't brought by a stork – that's just a story. Like all babies, you were made from a seed from Daddy and an egg from Mummy. Daddy's seed and Mummy's egg joined together in Mummy's tummy to make you, so you're very special – and a lovely mixture of Daddy and Mummy.

FOR AGES 6-8

A Daddy's seed, which are called sperm, are made in his testes, which are inside the special bag of skin, called a scrotum, hanging behind his penis. Millions of tiny sperm are being made there all the time and they are mixed with a white liquid called semen. Mummy's eggs grow inside her body in two egg-makers called ovaries. Every month Mummy's ovaries make an egg. When Mummy and Daddy made you, semen from Daddy's penis carried the sperm into Mummy's womb. One of the millions of sperm joined up with Mummy's egg to start a new baby – which was you.

FOR AGES 8-11

A You are here because Mum and Dad love one another and wanted to have a baby. To make a baby, Dad put his penis into Mum's vagina during sexual intercourse, and semen containing millions and millions of sperm – about 20 million sperm in one millilitre of semen – travelled up the vagina and through the womb, in the lower part of Mum's tummy, to join the egg. The scientific names for the egg and the womb are "ovum" and "uterus". The sperm swam very fast by lashing their long tails. To make sure the baby would be strong and healthy, only the fastest sperm joined up with the ovum to create the beginning of a new baby – which was you. While a baby is growing in the uterus, a woman is said to be "pregnant". It takes about nine months (40 weeks) for a baby to grow big enough to be born. Men can't have babies because they don't have proper wombs. Whether a baby is a boy or a girl depends on which sperm joins the egg, because some make boys and others girls. But usually no one knows which sperm has won the race until the baby is born. That's why it is so exciting when the baby comes out and we find out if it is a boy or a girl!

Does the baby grow inside you?

- *How does the baby live in your tummy?*
- *Why doesn't it fall out?* • *What can the baby do in your tummy?*
- *How does it breathe in your tummy?* • *What does it eat?*

Children are intrigued by the way a new baby develops in the womb – once they know it's there, they are just as fascinated by its progress as adults are. If you are expecting a new baby, you can help your older children share the experience as soon as the questions arise. Give them as much information as possible at every stage of the pregnancy, at the right level for their age and understanding.

—— WHAT'S BEHIND THIS QUESTION ——

A small child is simply trying to get a fix on a baby who's apparently locked away inside someone's body. It may be an addition to your family, or that of a friend – or your child may just have noticed a heavily pregnant woman in the supermarket, say, or at the doctor's.

These questions often go hand in hand with those on the previous pages, particularly, "How does the baby get in there?" Young children are quite satisfied with a simple answer. An older child will be curious about the things that particularly interest him – like what the baby eats or drinks, whether it can breathe, see or hear. Children over six may have begun to learn about these things at school in science and will be keen to apply their own knowledge to this unseen person.

—— GUIDELINES FOR YOUR ANSWERS ——

- This is an opportunity for a simple anatomy lesson. Use the illustrations here to help you explain how a baby grows and develops in the womb.
- Just start with broad strokes when answering a child under eight, gradually introducing more complex explanations with your eight- to eleven-year-old.

- It's reassuring to use a wall chart or pregnancy book with month-by-month illustrations to show your child how a baby develops as the weeks go by. Position the chart on the wall at your child's eye-level so that it is ready to be used as a reference at any time. An eight- or ten-year-old could be shown in more detail in a book.
- Whatever the age of your child, stress the fact that the unborn baby is happy, warm, content, well fed and can move about within a few weeks of implantation in the uterus. If the baby is a new brother- or sister-to-be, the aim is to help your child develop a relationship with the unborn baby so that he or she will be loved and welcomed when born. This way you can help the older child not to feel dethroned and jealous.
- Encourage a small child to go to sleep with his head resting near your tummy. Say things like, "I'm cuddling both my babies now." This will help your child to get used to the idea of another person in the family well before the birth, and will encourage him to accept the new baby more readily after he or she is born.

—— WHAT ELSE TO KNOW ——

- Talk about a forthcoming new baby all the time as "your baby", so that your child can feel that the new baby belongs just as much to him, but is shared with you as parents. This will help to instil a feeling of protection and ownership before the baby is born.
- Choose a name together as a family.
- Let your child feel the baby kick, and take your child with you to antenatal check-ups so that he can hear the heart beat or see the ultrasound scan as well.

Other things you may be asked...

- *Is it dark in your tummy?*
- *Does the baby move around?*
- *Can the baby see/hear anything in there?*
- *How big is the baby in your tummy?*

See also *Where did I come from? p. 12* • *How does the baby get out? p. 16*

FOR AGES 2–4

A Your baby has its own nest in Mummy's tummy. It is very warm, cosy and dark, and the baby is safe and happy.

FOR AGES 4–6

A Your baby grows in a special bag, called a womb, which is inside Mummy's tummy. It can't fall out because the bottom of the womb stays tight shut until the baby's ready to be born. Your baby is so happy, it kicks, sucks its thumb, opens and closes its eyes, or listens to the gurgles in Mummy's tummy. And sometimes it rests.

FOR AGES 6–8

A When the baby in the womb is a month old it is the size of your thumb nail. By the time the baby is six weeks old its heart is beating and its brain is forming too. The baby's arms and legs start from little buds and by 12 weeks the baby will have fingers and toes and look like a tiny human, but it's only about the length of my forefinger. It takes a long time – nine whole months – for a baby to grow big enough to be born. It doesn't need to eat, drink or breathe because food and oxygen come to it through a special tube attached to its tummy, and connected to its mother in the womb.

FOR AGES 8–11

A When a father's sperm first joins a mother's ovum the baby is the size of a pinhead, but it only takes about three months in the uterus for it to begin to look like a real baby. During these early weeks the baby goes through stages where it seems to have gills like a fish, and a little tail like a monkey. These are thought to be signs that humans evolved from sea creatures and then from apes. The baby's food and drink come from the mother's blood and reach the baby through the umbilical cord. You can see on your tummy where your cord was when you were inside Mum's uterus. The cord leads to a part of the uterus called the placenta where the baby's and mother's blood meet, so the baby takes in food and oxygen and gets rid of waste, such as carbon dioxide.

The fetus at 4 weeks – 4mm (⅙in)

At about 12 weeks – 9cm (3½in) long

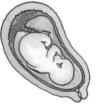
At about 20 weeks – 18.5cm (7⅓in)

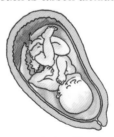
At about 32 weeks – 32cm (12in)

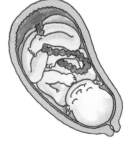
At about 40 weeks 35–37cm (14–15in) crown to rump

Q How does the baby get out?

- *How does the baby know when to be born?*
- *Does a doctor get the baby out?* • *Where does the baby come out?*
- *What happens when the baby is born?*

Children are as fascinated as adults by the process of birth, but they'll have little or no idea of how it all works. The younger they are, the more accepting they are of simple explanations, but if you are having your baby in hospital and your child is not accompanying you, you need to be clear about when your child can visit and when you and the baby will be coming home.

WHAT'S BEHIND THIS QUESTION

All children try to guess how the baby will come out – small children think that perhaps a mother will "unzip"! Older children are interested in the mechanics of birth and may ask to see the hole where the baby comes out. Some children may well have seen animals such as puppies or kittens being born, possibly on television, and they may want to know if it is the same for humans. Older children who have some knowledge of human biology may also want to know whether birth hurts the mother, and how it affects the baby.

GUIDELINES FOR YOUR ANSWERS

Try to be as accurate as possible, particularly if you are the parents-to-be. If you've decided to have your baby in hospital, entailing an enforced absence from your older child or children, it is important to let them know that you are not going to disappear for ever, and that the time before they can see you again will be short. That's why it's worth running through the stages of labour with your child so she has an idea of what will be happening when, and will understand that it could take a little while. Whether the questions arise because you or someone close to your child is pregnant, or whether the subject comes up simply from curiosity, use the illustrations here or in a pregnancy manual to help explain what happens. Try not to alarm your child with talk of pain and long labours.

If you are expecting a new baby, it's really helpful to take your child to see a pet cat or dog who has just given birth to kittens or puppies, if you know of one. When you go into labour, make it clear to your child that she can come and see you and her new baby as soon as possible after the birth, if she wants to.

WHAT ELSE TO KNOW

- If possible, take your child to the hospital before the birth and show her the delivery room and post-natal ward so that your child has a picture of where you will be.
- Let your child join in your preparation exercises. It makes it more fun for everyone and you can use them to help your child understand what's happening.
- If your child wants to see where the baby will come out, explain that the hole is too deep down. Show your child a picture instead.
- If you are lucky enough to be able to have your baby at home, make sure your older children are involved in the preparations and aren't excluded from the room if you all feel happy about it and there is no emergency. Discuss this in advance with your doctor and midwife.

Other things you may be asked...

- *Does it hurt to have a baby?*
- *How long does it take to be born?*
- *Will you still love me when the baby is born?*
- *Will the baby have hair and teeth?*
- *Why do you have to go to hospital?*

See also *Where did I come from? p. 12* • *Does the baby grow inside you? p. 14*

FOR AGES 2–4

After a while, your baby is too big for Mummy's tummy, so it has to be born. I'll still love you then.

FOR AGES 4–6

AYour baby is ready to be born when it needs more food than it can get from Mummy and it's too big to fit inside Mummy any more. Daddy's taking me to the hospital so the baby is born safely. Grandma will look after you, and Daddy will bring you to see me tomorrow. We'll all be at home in a couple of days with your new baby. I'll always love you.

FOR AGES 6–8

AThe womb is normally tight shut to keep the baby safe, but when the baby is ready to be born, the bottom of the womb – called the cervix – slowly stretches open like elastic and the strong womb muscles push the baby down the vagina and out from between Mummy's legs. This takes a few hours to happen. Human babies are born this way, and quite a few other baby animals too. When the baby is born he or she will probably cry a bit and will look around for the first time. Some babies have lots of hair, some only a little, and most babies don't grow teeth until they're about six months old.

FOR AGES 8–11

AThe baby knows when to be born when it grows too big for the amount of food coming from its mother. And the mother's body knows too because the baby is getting too big to fit in properly. The way out of the uterus is at the bottom, through the cervix, which is shut during pregnancy. When the baby is ready to be born the muscles of the uterus stretch the cervix open and push the baby down through the vagina – also known as the birth canal. Because the muscles are so strong it can be painful for the mother. The time when a baby is being pushed out is called "labour", which means work, because having a baby is hard work for the mother. Labour can last up to 18 hours or longer – because the baby has to be pushed down the birth canal, which stretches slowly so that it isn't damaged. Women having babies are looked after by doctors and special nurses called midwives. After birth the pains stop and the vagina and uterus shrink back to normal.

Q What is sex?

- *What is sexual intercourse?* • *What is making love?*
- *Do you (Mummy and Daddy) have sex?* • *Is sex nice?*
- *Why do people have sex?* • *Will I ever have sex?*

This is the one question that will inevitably be asked and that you should be ready to answer truthfully, whatever the age of your child. Being ready to answer your child's questions about sexual intercourse will help to foster a responsible and healthy attitude to sex when your child is old enough to be sexually active.

WHAT'S BEHIND THIS QUESTION

Few very young children ask this question unless they witness something overt, such as wandering into the bedroom while you are making love – and then the question would simply be, "What are you doing?" If a very young child does ask some of the questions above, it may be a danger sign of possible abuse (see p. 78), or may simply mean that he has been listening to older children. An older child asks these questions for three probable reasons:

- He may have heard or read the words "sex", "sexual intercourse", "making love", or similar, and is naturally curious. Your child wants a definition.
- Your child may have seen some aspect of sexual behaviour in a newspaper or magazine photograph, on TV or in a film or video. Again, your child may simply be curious, or possibly slightly alarmed, depending on the context of what he has seen, so find out the background circumstances.

Your child may pick up the idea that sex is a difficult or embarrassing subject for adults, who don't want to talk to children about it. In this situation the questions may be challenging, so stay cool.

Whether challenging or fact-finding, don't shy away from this question; instead, try to anticipate your child's concerns. Demystifying sex is the best way to avoid it becoming the object of furtive or smutty talk.

GUIDELINES FOR YOUR ANSWERS

- This question should always be looked at alongside the next two (*What's a vagina?* p. 20, and *What's a penis?* p. 22), as they are all very closely related. Choose your answers according to your child's needs.
- Answering questions such as these provides an opportunity to emphasize to children that sex should come from love and that with love comes responsibility: the responsibility to put the other person before themselves, never to coerce, pressure or force, and to have respect for others and for themselves.
- Pre-school children only ever need the simplest explanations about sex. While you may be trembling in anticipation of the next question, they will just change the subject, or say, "Thanks, Dad", and run off to play.

WHAT ELSE TO KNOW

- Think of each question your child asks as an opportunity to convey your standards and values and to help your child feel loved and well-informed.
- Remember there's rarely need for detailed information about the mechanics of sex for a child under eight.
- Try to anticipate your child's concerns. Remember that sex is also about self-control and abstinence and you should school your child about these qualities.

Other things you may be asked...

- *What is "getting laid"/"having it off"/"bonking"?*
- *Do you make a baby every time you have sex?*
- *Do you only have sex in bed?*
- *Why do people kiss and cuddle?*
- *Do you stop having sex when you're old?*

See also *Where did I come from? p. 12* • *What's a vagina? p. 20* • *What's a penis? p. 22* • *What's a contraceptive? p. 30*

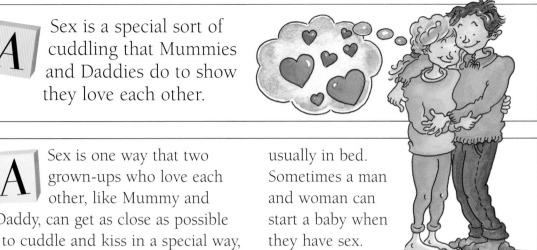

Sex is a special sort of cuddling that Mummies and Daddies do to show they love each other.

Sex is one way that two grown-ups who love each other, like Mummy and Daddy, can get as close as possible to cuddle and kiss in a special way, usually in bed. Sometimes a man and woman can start a baby when they have sex.

Sex is one of the ways in which two grown-up people can show that they love each other. Sex is the time when they can make each other feel happy and wonderful. When we talk about sex in this way it is short for "sexual intercourse". There are lots of slang words for sex but they're not polite. During sexual intercourse, a man's penis gets stiff and he puts it inside his partner's vagina, which feels nice. Having sex can start a baby, but usually it doesn't because grown-ups generally have sex as a way of showing how much they love each other, even when they are quite old.

Your sex can mean whether you are a girl or a boy – your "gender". But sex is also short for "sexual intercourse", which is how grown-ups like Mum and Dad can make someone they love feel very happy and good about themselves; that's why we call it making love. During sexual intercourse, a man puts his penis inside a woman's vagina, and they feel good. The feeling becomes more and more exciting until it reaches a climax, when the man's sperm spurts – or ejaculates – into the woman's vagina. You don't have to take your clothes off, but most people like to because it helps to get really close, so sex happens most often in bed when two people don't wear clothes. There are lots of different ways that two people can have sex, so long as it is comfortable for both of them. Although having sexual intercourse can make a baby, many people have sex simply because they love each other and it feels nice, so they use contraceptives which prevent a baby from starting. People usually wait until they are grown-up before they begin having sexual relationships, but no-one should have sex with anyone else until they feel they are ready for it.

● *Does sex feel nice? p. 34*

Q What's a vagina?

- *What's a vagina for?* ● *Why haven't I got a penis?*
- *What's a penis for?* ● *Why don't boys have a vagina?*
- *When will I be able to have a baby?* ● *What are breasts for?*

All children want to identify with other children of the same gender. They are concerned not to be taken for the opposite gender, so they want to know about all similarities and all differences. Girls want to know about the things that are special to them. But boys also need to know, so if you can, discuss the answers here and those for "What's a penis?" (p. 22) with sons and daughters together, so that each gender knows about the other.

WHAT'S BEHIND THIS QUESTION

Girls start to identify with other girl children from an early age, and will look for signs of similarity between girls, and features that distinguish them from boys. However, very few girls under the age of four will be interested enough to ask questions, mainly because they think everybody else is made the way they are. From school age, girls begin to look for differences between children and between grown men and women.

The presence of a penis is such an obvious difference that children use it naturally: "Is this doll a girl or a boy? Where's the penis?" There's no harm in a mother showing her daughter that she doesn't have a penis; it is the best kind of reassurance and will make your daughter feel confident about herself – she is the same as Mummy! Equally, a daughter will often compare herself with her father, note the differences and want to know why they occur.

GUIDELINES FOR YOUR ANSWERS

● Don't ever scold your child for being sexually curious about people of the opposite sex; satisfy that curiosity by answering questions frankly and honestly.

● Much was once made of the Freudian theory that girls suffer from "penis envy" – that they are innately jealous that they do not have a penis. This may not be literally true, but girls do have to wait a long time before developing obvious signs of their own sexuality – their breasts. But they have two – a source of pride.

● If you have sons as well as daughters, include them in your conversation. Boys need to know about girls because knowledge and understanding will help to instil in them a sense of responsibility and understanding of girls' and women's needs from an early age.

WHAT ELSE TO KNOW

● Any girl will explore herself during her first and second years. This is part of normal infant development. Be tolerant and never ask your baby to refrain from touching herself – accept that it is normal and pleasurable. It isn't "dirty".

● Your daughter may start enquiring specifically about sex from the age of six; she may play "mothers and fathers" when she imitates you and may want to explore boys' bodies. Relax, this is normal, but keep an eye on it to make sure it is safe; in particular, watch that she does not push any object up into herself.

● Your nine- to ten-year-old daughter could become shy about asking questions, so encourage her: mothers particularly should try to be open. Tell her what developing as a woman was like for you.

Other things you may be asked...

- ■ *Do boys have breasts?*
- ■ *Does urine come out of the vagina?*
- ■ *What's a clitoris?*
- ■ *When did you/Mum get your/her breasts?*
- ■ *What are ovaries?*
- ■ *What's a womb?*

See also *Where did I come from? p. 12* ● *What is sex? p. 18* ● *What's a penis? p. 20* ● *What does puberty mean? p. 26*

FOR AGES 2–4

Few children under the age of four will ask this question because they take their anatomy for granted. But if your child does begin to notice and ask about gender differences, base your answers on those given for the 4–6 age group, below.

FOR AGES 4–6

A The vagina is a tube that goes up into your body from the opening between your legs. Boys and men don't have vaginas; they have penises instead. The vagina is the tube that male seeds travel along to make a baby, and the vagina stretches open so the baby can be born. Breasts are for making milk to feed a newborn baby. You'll start growing breasts when you're about 12, like Mummy did.

FOR AGES 6–8

A Every girl and woman has a vagina, while all boys and men have a penis. A vagina is a stretchy tube that starts between your legs and goes up into your body. Girls also have a clitoris, which is a bit like a penis, but it is small and doesn't stick out much. A clitoris can get stiff like a penis, and when it does, it feels tingly and nice. Sperm comes out through a man's penis, in semen. The vagina produces fluid to keep it comfortable, specially during sexual intercourse. Girls have a small hole near to their clitoris for passing urine. A girl is able to have a baby from about the age of 13, but most women choose to wait until they're grown up before having a baby.

FOR AGES 8–11

A When a man and a woman, like Mum and Dad, want to have sexual intercourse, the vagina becomes moist and wet to make it easy for the penis to enter, and it feels very nice – in fact it is so enjoyable that both partners may have an orgasm. When a man has an orgasm, the semen, which contains sperm, spurts into the vagina – this is called an ejaculation. A woman doesn't ejaculate when she has an orgasm but her vagina does become more moist. All penises get stiff and erect from time to time. Sometimes your clitoris probably gets hard too and you may want to touch it because it feels nice. That's OK, it's quite normal and most girls and women do it. The vagina leads up into the womb (uterus), which is where a baby develops. The ovaries, which produce an egg every month, are well protected inside a woman's body, while a man's testes hang outside his body in the scrotum to keep cool.

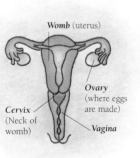

Womb (uterus)

Ovary (where eggs are made)

Cervix (Neck of womb)

Vagina

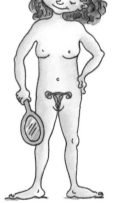

• *What is a period? p. 28* • *What's masturbation? p. 32* • *Does sex feel nice? p. 34*

Q What's a penis?

- *Why have I got a penis?* • *Why don't girls have a penis?*
- *Why does my penis get bigger/harder?* • *What are testicles for?*
- *Why hasn't Daddy got breasts?* • *What's a vagina?*

Like girls' questions about their anatomy, boys want to know about the things that are special to them. Most of these questions are from the boy's point of view, but girls will also want to be informed about boys to help them understand why boys and girls like and do different things. If possible, discuss the answers given here and those for "What's a vagina?" (p. 20) with your sons and daughters together, so that each knows about the other.

WHAT'S BEHIND THIS QUESTION

None of these questions are prurient – in fact, they are intelligent. From the age of two and a half, boys are very interested in the fact that they are boys, so they are curious about all their male features. They want to be like other boys and don't want to be mistaken for girls. By the age of about five, boys start comparing themselves to girls, mainly to find differences. Your son will also want to know if he and his father are made the same way – he loves identifying with his father. Later, when he either learns about or experiences a wet dream, he'll want to be reassured that it is normal and if other boys and men he knows have them too – even Dad.

GUIDELINES FOR YOUR ANSWERS

- One of the best ways to reassure a boy that he is normal is to let him compare his penis with his father's, and to find out that it does the same things as his does.
- Four-year-old boys are intrigued by their genitals, because they have years of experience of this interesting part of them which squirts and tingles and that they can get hold of, but now they want to know more. This is normal; don't discourage it. Be laid back, but also

positive: permit your young son's self-stimulation and sexual curiosity. Accept that your child is a sexual being who feels aroused through exploring his body. Never speak harshly to him about this; ignore what he is doing or distract him with another activity.
- Although children under five years of age are interested in their genitals, and those of others, they are in fact unlikely to ask these questions, because they usually take their anatomy for granted.

WHAT ELSE TO KNOW

- From birth to 18 months it's normal for boys to experience penile erections and to touch and play with their penises. By the age of three your toddler is still very interested in genitals, and in urine and faeces.
- It's normal for six-year-olds to express concrete interest in sexuality by playing "doctor", or "mothers and fathers". As long as it is safe, try to accept that this is not an erotic game as you would interpret it.
- Questions about the function of the penis lead naturally to questions from both boys and girls about the vagina. Refer back to the questions and answers on pages 20 and 21, but remember that you need never show a child a real vagina. Most children will accept that it is private. However, by seven or eight, you can show your child a simple drawing. In answer to questions from a nine- or ten-year-old boy, a father can explain what a vagina feels like to him.

Other things you may be asked...

- *Why haven't I got a vagina?*
- *Do all boys have the same kind of penis?*
- *Does Daddy's penis get hard too?*
- *What happens inside my testicles?*
- *What's a foreskin?*
- *What's ejaculation?*

See also *What is sex? p. 18* • *What's a vagina? p. 20* • *What does puberty mean? p. 26* • *What's masturbation? p. 32*

Children under the age of four will rarely ask this question because they take their anatomy for granted. But if your child begins to ask about gender differences, base your answers on those given for the 4–6 age group, below.

A All boys and men have penises. A penis does two things: it gets rid of water and other things that you don't need in your body in urine, and when a man is grown-up it helps him to make a baby. All penises grow hard now and then, especially if you touch or hold them. Daddy's penis is exactly like yours, except it's quite a bit bigger.

A Most of the time your penis is used to get rid of urine, but a penis can also become hard, so that when a man is grown up it can go easily into a woman's vagina to put sperm right inside, so a baby might be formed. A vagina is a stretchy tube that starts between a woman's legs and goes up inside her body. Your penis is very sensitive and it probably gets bigger sometimes without your being able to do anything about it – as if it was on automatic pilot – but it feels nice. Girls and women don't have penises. They have a clitoris which is small but also grows and tingles, a bit like a penis does. Near the clitoris is a small hole where urine comes out.

A An erection is the word for a penis which has become stiff. It is perfectly normal to have erections – it's part of growing up. By the time you're about 12 or so, your testes will be making a lot of sperm day and night. When the sperm has collected, it just has to get out, so you might have a "wet dream", which just means that sperm comes out when you are asleep. That's normal and natural, and most boys have wet dreams. Testes are sperm factories, and in order for sperm production to go smoothly, the temperature of the testes must be lower than that of the rest of your body. That's why they hang outside the body in the scrotum. The foreskin is the circle of very flexible skin that protects the tip of your penis. The foreskin is sometimes removed for religious reasons when a boy is still a baby; occasionally it is done for medical reasons. It doesn't make any difference to the way the penis works.

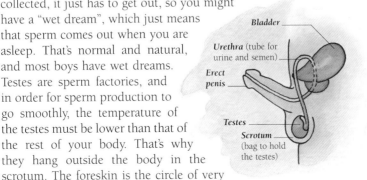

Bladder

Urethra (tube for urine and semen)

Erect penis

Testes

Scrotum (bag to hold the testes)

• *Does sex feel nice?* p. 34

Q Why can't I take my clothes off?

- *Can I get in the bath with you?* • *Do I have to put my clothes on?*
- *Is it all right to walk around with no clothes on?*
- *Why do you and Daddy sometimes have no clothes on?*

The subject of nudity is unfortunately often surrounded by taboos, but there needn't be any inhibition within a family with children under eleven. However, try to make young children aware that some people, particularly from an older generation, such as grandparents, may see things differently, and that it is polite to respect their views and behave accordingly.

WHAT'S BEHIND THIS QUESTION

Up to the age of seven or eight children are quite unselfconscious about their own or anyone else's nudity. If they learn to be prudish at all, they learn it from adults who are shifty about nakedness. To most children, nudity is quite normal and they may find it difficult to understand why limits need be set. However, even if you as a family are unconcerned about nudity, others – their own friends' parents just as much as those of an older generation – may not be. When they experience these differing viewpoints, your children are likely to question them.

GUIDELINES FOR YOUR ANSWERS

- Try not to programme your children with your own hang-ups about nudity, if you have them. Your younger children will be naturally unembarrassed; take your lead from them.
- At around eight or nine, however, some children (particularly girls) may give you very clear signals that they are no longer comfortable about exposing their bodies. You may find that your daughter starts shutting her bedroom door or puts a "KEEP OUT" sign on it; she may want to bolt the bathroom door for the first

time, and cover herself up when changing for swimming or sport. When this happens, respect her need for privacy. It is part of the beginnings of sexual awareness that precedes the onset of puberty. At the same time, help her maintain a positive attitude to her appearance to avoid problems with low self-esteem later.
- Try to be consistent about nudity. For instance, if you were in the habit of getting into the bath with your baby, it is not a very good idea just a year or two later to become coy about showing your body. Not only could you confuse your child, but also encourage furtiveness, secrecy and loss of trust in you.

WHAT ELSE TO KNOW

- The fewer the limits set, the better. My own children followed me into the lavatory until they were five or six years old and felt free to come into the bathroom or bedroom at any time while I was dressing. Some parents may well feel shy about this but my primary concern was to make myself available to my children at all times, as well as to make them feel comfortable with nakedness and therefore with their own bodies.
- Of course, your child also will have to learn that outside your home others may not be so open about nudity; you may need to explain that it's good manners not to embarrass other people. What is perfectly acceptable at home may not be possible or advisable elsewhere. In the main, children understand these differences and will happily accommodate them once you explain the reasons for them.

Other things you may be asked...

- *Does it matter if boys and girls both have no clothes on?*
- *Can I come into the bathroom with you?*
- *Why does Granny mind when I take my clothes off?*
- *Why does John's Mummy say it's rude to have no clothes on?*
- *Why does Karen get upset when I take my clothes off?*

See also *What's a vagina? p. 20* • *What's a penis? p. 22* • *What does puberty mean? p. 26*

A Of course I don't mind if you take your clothes off so long as you don't get cold. But if Granny's looking after you and she'd rather you kept your clothes on, it's best to do as she wants because we don't want to hurt her feelings.

A I know it feels fresh to take your clothes off, and Daddy and I often walk around without clothes on when we get up. And you can come into the bathroom if you want to talk to me when I'm in there. But sometimes people are shy and it's not fair to make them feel uncomfortable, so get dressed for their sake.

A It's okay to play in Lucy's garden without clothes because her Mum doesn't mind. But if you play at Karen's it would be better to keep your clothes on because Karen is shy and her Mum doesn't like it. People from some places wear hardly any clothes at all, but others think it's better to cover their whole bodies, so when we're with other people we should respect their feelings about this. Daddy and I don't mind if you see us without clothes sometimes at home because we like our bodies and it's nice not to have clothes covering them for a change.

A I do understand if you worry about someone seeing you when you're changing for swimming, and that you don't want your brother coming into the bathroom any more when you're there. I remember feeling exactly the same myself at your age. It's part of growing up to begin to think you need more privacy. But remember he hasn't got to that stage yet so we could make a notice to put on your door saying, "This is Jo's room!" or "KEEP OUT – PRIVATE". We'll put a lock on the bathroom door too.

Q What does puberty mean?

- *Why is Michael's voice going funny?* • *What are hormones?*
- *When will I start to grow breasts?* • *What's adolescence?*
- *Why am I growing hair between my legs?*

When your child starts asking about puberty, take him seriously because it's an indication that he's thinking about growing up. Children under six will rarely mention puberty as such, but their questions might arise from seeing changes in older children close to your family.

WHAT'S BEHIND THIS QUESTION

This is one of the biggest and most challenging questions from a child, because he probably suspects it has something to do with sexuality. A younger child who actually includes the word "puberty" in a question will have heard the word used somewhere, but a child over six will know that children's bodies change as they get older, and will want to know about these changes.

GUIDELINES FOR YOUR ANSWERS

- Never dodge your child's questions about puberty.
- Find a good starting point by asking, "What particularly interests you about puberty?" or, "Have you heard something about puberty already?"

- By the time your child is ten, you could include yourself by sharing your own experience of puberty.
- Never make fun of your child, and respect his need for privacy. This will encourage him to come to you when older to ask you more difficult questions, knowing you'll never criticize or judge.

WHAT ELSE TO KNOW

- A girl of nine or ten may begin to show early signs of puberty such as breast development and body hair, so she needs to know what to expect in good time.
- The best way to prepare your child for puberty is to give him accurate information on all aspects of the changes that happen to boys and girls, including menstruation and fertility, wet dreams and masturbation.

Other things you may be asked...

- *When did you start puberty?*
- *What does fertile mean?*
- *When did you start to shave?*

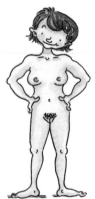
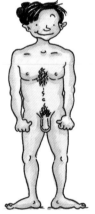
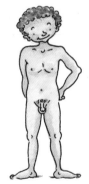

At age 6–7 girls are flat-chested and hairless. They lose rounded baby tummies, but have no "waistline".

At age 10–11 many girls will be showing breast development and pubic hair will start to grow.

By age 14–15 girls' bodies will be rounded, breasts enlarged, and body hair will have grown.

By age 15–17 boys' shoulders will have broadened, the genitals enlarged and facial hair appeared.

At age 12–14 boys' voices begin to break, and body hair to grow around the genitals and underarms.

At age 6–7 boys' bodies are like girls' in shape and the penis and testes are small and hairless.

See also *Where did I come from? p. 12* • *What is sex? p. 18* • *What is a period? p. 28* • *What's masturbation? p. 32*

Children under the age of four will rarely ask this question unless they hear the word used by other people. If a mature three-and-a-half year old child raises the subject, base your answers on those I have given for the 4–6 age group, below.

A Puberty is a time when lots of exciting things change in your body and you really begin to grow up. It's when girls start to grow breasts and boys' voices get deeper, and boys and girls sometimes get spots, but puberty won't happen to you until you're a lot older.

A Puberty is the time during your teens when you grow tall and your body begins to change shape. Girls grow breasts, and boys' shoulders get broader and more muscular. Girls start their monthly periods which show that their bodies are getting ready to have a baby when they are older, and they grow hair under their arms and between their legs. Boys start making sperm in their testes and grow hair around their penises and testes, under their arms and on their chest, legs and face as well, so eventually boys have to start shaving. Their voices get much lower too, like mine/Dad's.

A At puberty your body starts to grow really fast, inside and out. Girls usually start to change a couple of years before boys. Special chemicals called hormones, produced by the body, help change girls' shape so their waists get smaller, their breasts grow, their hips and thighs get rounder and they start their monthly periods, usually around the age of 12 or 13. From then on a girl is fertile – she could have a baby. Hormones produced in boys' bodies make their muscles develop and their shoulders get broader, and they have erections and wet dreams. The penis and scrotum get bigger, and these are all signs that sperm are beginning to be produced and a boy becomes fertile – able to father children. Boys' voices start to get deeper – or break – when they are about 13 or 14, and they may need to start shaving when they're about 16. Both boys and girls grow hair between their legs and under their arms, and may get spots. And everyone produces more sweat, so it's a good idea to have a bath or to shower frequently. The time when these changes happen is called "adolescence". During adolescence, it's normal for boys and girls to feel a bit moody – this isn't really very surprising when you think about all the important and exciting things that are happening at that time!

For boys: "I might start shaving when I'm about 16 and my voice might break when I'm 14, like Dad's."

For girls: "I might need my first bra when I'm 12, like Mum did."

Q What is a period?

- *Why are you/is Mummy bleeding?* ● *Why don't boys have periods?*
- *Do periods last a long time?* ● *When will I start my periods?*
- *What's menstruation?* ● *Will I ever stop having periods?*

Your children's questions about menstruation need to be handled positively. Young children may equate bleeding with pain and injury, so they need to be reassured that it's normal. Older girls and boys should all be prepared for this change in girls' bodies, but girls need more detail.

WHAT'S BEHIND THIS QUESTION

Periods could start to be part of children's conversation around the age of seven, although a younger child might hear the word much earlier. I remember my four-year-old son asking me what "temperstation" was, after he heard me telling my husband I was menstruating. Children often approach the subject furtively, as though it was something dirty and distasteful, because many adults can be secretive about menstruation, treating it as taboo. For this reason you may find that their questions about it are a bit challenging.

It is important to be open with your child from her first question, no matter how young she is. Children are quick to pick up signs of unwillingness to talk and will take advantage of this if you aren't candid. The subject may arise if a younger child finds tampons or sanitary towels in the bathroom or notices bloodstains on underwear, especially if you allow your child into the bathroom with you. Seeing menstrual blood can

be quite alarming to a young child, who may associate it with an injury and might think Mummy has hurt herself or is ill, so it is essential to give her immediate reassurance that everything is natural and normal.

GUIDELINES FOR YOUR ANSWERS

- Girls need to be aware that it is perfectly normal for periods to start anywhere between the ages 10 and 15.
- Girls should be reassured that the blood may be brown rather than red to start with, that early periods may not be regular, and that there may be abdominal pain, which is easily treated with painkillers.
- Try to emphasize to boys that they should be sympathetic to girls and women who are menstruating; explain that periods can be painful and may make girls and women a bit moody.
- Avoid negative connotations – don't say, "That's when I'm poorly", or refer to menstruation as "the curse". Make sure children know that life goes on as normal.

WHAT ELSE TO KNOW

- Girls who begin to menstruate without being forewarned – and many still do – can react badly. They may suffer profound shock, think they're ill or, worse, dying, then may grow up to feel ambivalent about their sexuality and have difficulty with relationships.
- Help your daughter by telling her in good time – a likely start date is the age that you (her mother) began.
- When she is about ten years old, explain to your daughter how sanitary towels and tampons are used.

Other things you may be asked...

- *Does everyone know when you've got a period?*
- *How do you stop the bleeding?*
- *Do periods hurt?*
- *What's a tampon for?*
- *Can I do P.E. when I have a period?*

Press-on towel
Best when periods become regular.

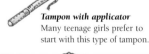

Tampon with applicator
Many teenage girls prefer to start with this type of tampon.

Tampon
The simplest internal towel for active teenage girls and women.

Mini-towel
Slim, fitted towel is good for scanty periods.

See also *Where did I come from? p. 12* ● *What's a vagina? p. 20* ● *What does puberty mean? p. 26*

A A period is the time every month when Mummy's body bleeds and reminds her she can have a baby if she wants to. Don't worry, Mummy's not ill and she hasn't hurt herself.

A A period and menstruation are just different words for the same thing – it's the time every 28 days or so that most women's bodies shows that they're able to have a baby – that they're fertile. Girls normally start having periods when they are about 12 or 13, at the time of their lives that's called puberty, when lots of changes happen to their bodies to get them ready for having a baby one day. During a period a girl bleeds through her vagina for a few days every month – but it's quite normal; it happens to most girls and women every month, except when they're going to have a baby. During a period, a woman wears a sanitary towel inside her pants. Most girls start with these, but later they might wear a towel inside, called a tampon. Their mothers or a nurse show them how to use it.

A Getting a period or menstruating means that every month the hormones from a girl's ovaries get her body ready to become pregnant, though of course most of the time she doesn't. Most women don't choose to have a baby until they're in their late twenties. One of the hormones, called oestrogen, makes the lining of the womb thick and healthy in preparation for a baby. If a woman doesn't become pregnant, the womb no longer needs to be ready to receive a baby, so the lining just comes away and it bleeds. When the bleeding stops the whole cycle starts again. Boys and men don't get periods because they don't have an actual womb. Nobody else knows when a girl has a period and she can do everything she does the rest of the time, including sports – even swimming if she's old enough to wear a tampon. Sanitary towels and tampons are very comfortable and don't get in the way. You just have to remember to change them often. Some girls may get a tummy ache during periods but it doesn't usually last long. Women stop having periods when they're about 50 because the hormones controlling menstruation stop being produced.

Tampon

Sanitary towel

Q What's a contraceptive?

- *Why don't you have a baby every time you have sex?*
- *How do you stop having a baby?* • *What's "the pill"?*
- *What's a condom/rubber?* • *What's safe sex?*

Although questions about contraception are unlikely to come from children under six, once your child is at school there could well be an older child who thinks it's funny to produce a condom in the playground for a joke. It is important to be open, because accurate information about methods of contraception is essential well before your child is likely to be sexually active. Knowledge of contraception encourages responsible sexual conduct.

WHAT'S BEHIND THIS QUESTION

If your child asks about contraception, he probably knows quite a bit about sex already. Some of it may be accurate but most will have been acquired as half-truths in the playground – almost certainly exaggerated, and undoubtedly mystifying. In any event, to understand contraception a child needs to know the basics of sex and reproduction, so ensure he has that understanding first by asking more detailed questions like, "Where did you first hear about contraception?" or, "What kind of contraceptives were you thinking about?" If the questions are about specific types of contraceptive, ask specific questions like, "Have you seen a rubber?", "Was someone talking about condoms today?" or, "How did you hear about safe sex?" This will help both to guide you to the source of the query and to give you an idea of your child's present level of knowledge.

GUIDELINES FOR YOUR ANSWERS

- There's no specific age when children should have information about contraception – it depends on your child. You may have to give explanations earlier to a sexually aware daughter than a shy son – or vice versa.

- Although younger children are unlikely to raise this subject in the form of the questions given above, it may well crop up in the course of another conversation, for instance about where babies come from.
- Don't shy away from questions about contraception or make the mistake of thinking it encourages sexual activity. It does the opposite.
- Where possible, show your child the different types of contraceptive and how they work – the drawings below will help, but better still, show them the real thing, or promise to do it later and keep your promise.

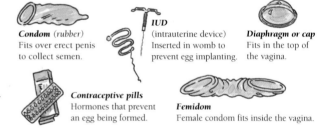

Condom *(rubber)*
Fits over erect penis to collect semen.

IUD
(intrauterine device) Inserted in womb to prevent egg implanting.

Diaphragm or cap
Fits in the top of the vagina.

Contraceptive pills
Hormones that prevent an egg being formed.

Femidom
Female condom fits inside the vagina.

WHAT ELSE TO KNOW

- There is no reason why you should not demonstrate to children over eight how a condom works – boys *and* girls – by putting it over a banana. Make a game of it – blow it up like a balloon. It's a sure way of demystifying something that often becomes a focus among children for uninformed discussion about sex.
- A discussion of contraception needs to include the unwelcome outcomes of sex: unwanted pregnancy, AIDS, herpes and other sexually transmitted diseases.

Other things you may be asked...

- *How do contraceptives work?*
- *How do you put on a condom?*
- *Is there a rubber for girls?*
- *Where do you get contraceptives from?*
- *What happens if you don't take your pill?*

See also *Where did I come from? p. 12* • *What is sex? p. 18* • *What's a vagina? p. 20* • *What's a penis? p. 22*

A People who love each other, like Mummy and Daddy, use contraceptives to stop them from making a baby until they think they are really ready to have one.

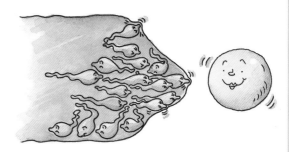

A A contraceptive stops a baby from being made when a man and a woman have sex. There are lots of kinds of contraceptive, some for women and some for men, which work in different ways. The types of contraceptive that are used most often are the pill and the condom. A woman can take a pill every day which she gets from the doctor. The pills stop eggs being released from the woman's ovaries. If she stops taking the pills she could start a baby the next month, so a couple must always use another sort of contraceptive when a woman stops taking the pill if they don't want a baby. A man can wear a condom, which he puts on his penis when it is stiff. It catches the sperm so they don't go inside the woman's body. Condoms also stop people from passing diseases to each other when they have sex. When a man uses a condom the couple are both safe from catching a type of really bad illness, like AIDS.

A Contraceptives prevent pregnancies, which is the reason why any man and woman who are having sex MUST use a contraceptive if they don't want a baby. Nothing else will do. When a couple has sex, they share the responsibility for contraception and usually decide together what to use. A woman can take the contraceptive pill every day, or she can have an IUD (intrauterine device) put inside her womb by a doctor to stop a baby starting. Or she can wear a rubber disc, called a cap or diaphragm, which fits inside her vagina to stop sperm going into the womb. Men can wear condoms, which stop sperm from going into a woman's body. Wearing condoms is part of "safe sex", which means having sex in a way that stops certain diseases being passed on. There are also condoms for women, which fit all the way up inside the vagina. Lots of different shops sell condoms, but it's best to get most other contraceptives from a doctor or a family planning clinic, which you can usually visit at any time. But Mum and Dad are ready to talk to you about contraception whenever you want to.

● *What is a period? p. 28* ● *What is AIDS? p. 92*

Q What's masturbation?

- *Can I touch myself down there?* • *What's mutual masturbation?*
- *Is it dirty to touch myself down there?* • *Do you masturbate?*
- *What does "playing with yourself" mean?* • *What's wanking?*

Masturbation is one of the most difficult questions for many parents to face – not because the subject is in itself complicated, but because of their own attitudes to it. Your child has the right to be relaxed about masturbation. Being clear in your own mind that masturbation is normal and beneficial will help to dispel the myths that surround it.

WHAT'S BEHIND THIS QUESTION

Your child may well start hearing the word at school and begin to wonder what it means. She may also have heard from other children all sorts of myths about masturbation being dirty and having dreadful consequences. Most of these myths originate from anxious adults who can't cope with the idea of quite young children stimulating themselves sexually. So your child's questions about masturbation, or about "touching" or "rubbing", probably arise because someone has told them off or remarked on it.

GUIDELINES FOR YOUR ANSWERS

- This is a vexed question for many parents because of misunderstandings starting in their own childhood. Masturbation is not bad in itself; treat it as a normal part of growing up and don't plant the seeds of shame.
- Tolerate or ignore masturbation; if questions arise, answer them simply and factually; agree that "It feels nice to touch your penis", but set limits: "This is something we do in private." If your child absent-mindedly masturbates in public, treat it as you would bad manners or unthoughtfulness: "Those people would be more comfortable if you didn't do that here."

- Up to the age of five, one child touching another is nearly always innocent. Make sure that one child is not an unwilling victim and that they are not trying to put things into themselves. The exception to this would be a child who has been abused when very small.
- If a child talks about someone who is significantly older and more developed touching her, you should treat this as a danger signal. Calmly ascertain exactly what has happened (if anything) and be vigilant when she's in the company of that person in the future.

WHAT ELSE TO KNOW

- It is important to remember that all babies explore their genitals from about four months. This is a continuous process of development and children never naturally stop touching or feeling themselves. As they get older they may realize that touching their genitals is pleasurable, but a young child's masturbation has nothing to do with sex as we think of it; it stems from a desire to explore and understand.
- As it's normal for children to touch their genitals, don't be surprised if your child reacts defensively to any suggestion that it is "dirty" or "harmful". It isn't – masturbation is only harmful if you react negatively to it.
- Masturbation is a healthy and natural way to release tension. The only time I would be concerned is if a child were masturbating habitually to escape from a horrible world, because he was being emotionally deprived. A child like this needs help; the way to correct it is to give love, not punishment.

Other things you may be asked...

- *I let Susan touch my penis. Is that alright?*
- *Can Richard touch me down there?*
- *Is masturbation bad for you?*
- *Does everyone masturbate?*
- *Why does my penis stick up when I hold it?*

See also *What is sex? p. 18* • *Does sex feel nice? p. 34* • *Why can't I talk to strangers? p. 76*

Children under the age of four will rarely ask this question because exploring their bodies is normal and unremarkable.

If a mature three-and-a-half year-old raises the subject in any way, base your answers on the 4–6 age group, below.

A It doesn't matter if you touch yourself there, but it's best to do it at home. If a little friend has touched you, it doesn't matter, so long as you didn't mind, but if you don't like it, say no and tell me. Big children and grownups must never touch you there and you must tell me even if they say that it is bad to tell or a secret.

A It doesn't matter if you touch yourself down there, most people do, boys and girls as well as grown-ups, because it feels nice. A few people may say that it's wrong – it isn't at all, but we usually do it in private. The big word for it is masturbation, and it's so normal that everyone does it sometimes.

A Masturbation and wanking mean the same thing – wanking is just a slang word for it. It means touching or rubbing the clitoris in girls or the penis in boys – and it's perfectly normal. It feels nice and most people do it – grown-ups too. It's never bad for you and nothing terrible will happen to you if you do it, but it's best to do it in private. You won't go deaf or blind or get spots or grow hair on the palms of your hands – and you can tell whoever told you those things that they are just silly stories and they simply aren't true. Sometimes a boy's penis or a girl's clitoris just seem to get hard and to tingle for no reason at all, and it's a normal reaction to want to rub it, which can feel very nice. But if you don't want to touch yourself down there that's OK too. When boys and girls get to be a bit older, they may have an orgasm from masturbating. When an older boy has an orgasm he ejaculates and semen comes out of his penis. An orgasm is a very exciting feeling that spreads over your whole body; afterwards you may feel a bit sleepy.

Q Does sex feel nice?

- *What is ejaculation?* ● *What's an orgasm?* ● *What's oral sex?*

- *Do you have an orgasm every time ?* ● *Do girls ejaculate?*

- *Does everyone have orgasms?* ● *What's "coming"?*

As children get older and more knowing, they will begin to ask more searching questions, especially if they hear slang words used about sex among their friends. Answering these questions frankly and accurately could be difficult for you because of your sensibilities and feelings about privacy, but for your children's sake try to deal with them coolly.

WHAT'S BEHIND THIS QUESTION

I feel that these questions are mainly the province of the older age groups. Accept that your child is quite worldly by the time he starts looking for answers to questions like these. He is really searching for good, solid, accurate information. Any child who asks these questions can deal with detailed explanations of sexual intercourse – in fact these questions may well arise out of conversations you've already had about sex, and your child is showing his trust in you if he brings you further questions about sexual subjects.

GUIDELINES FOR YOUR ANSWERS

● Don't cop out. You're letting your child down if you use an excuse like, "I don't know how to describe it – I can't find the words." The truth of the matter is you don't have to. Just keep it simple.
● Although older children are the ones most likely to raise these issues, a child under six may hear a word like "orgasm" spoken, and could ask what it means. As with other questions about sexuality, you need only provide the simplest explanation.
● Even your knowing 11-year-old may be a bit frightened by some of the information, so watch closely for signs of anxiety and reassure him that he'll find out that

it's normal and natural when it finally happens to him – but that it's unlikely to be for a long time yet.
● Be simple, non-judgmental and tonelessly factual, as if you were describing the weather. Check that you're on the right lines by saying, "Is this the sort of thing you want to know?", so you don't blunder on unnecessarily.

WHAT ELSE TO KNOW

● I would have felt delinquent if I hadn't given you some help in how to answer this and related questions. "What is 69?" is only included to cover all eventualities. If you're uncomfortable, don't touch on such subjects spontaneously, but if your child faces you with them, use the answers opposite to help you. You'll never need to use all the information here – pick and choose what's appropriate at the time.
● Giving the information simply and straightforwardly in the way I have described is not salacious; more and better information will give your child the best chance to manage the choppy waters of puberty. Children who are given information about sex by their own parents are better able to act responsibly in the future. They will have the strength to stand their ground, say "no" (and to more than sex, too), so respect their needs and try wherever possible to stress that enjoyment of sex should be mutual between two people when each has the responsibility for the other's pleasure. They need to know that people mustn't be used.

Other things you may be asked...

- *What's a blow job?*
- *What's mutual masturbation?*
- *What does "69" mean?*
- *Do boys/girls have orgasms?*
- *What's anal sex?*
- *Do men do oral sex with women too?*

See also *What is sex? p. 18* ● *What's masturbation? p. 32*

Children under six are unlikely to ask this question. However, if they do hear this or a similar word spoken and ask what it means, simply say: "An orgasm's a nice feeling that starts deep inside your body and makes you feel really good."

An orgasm is a very nice feeling that people get after they have been rubbing or touching their clitoris or penis. You probably won't have this feeling until you're quite a bit older – say 13 or 14. Men and women have this feeling as part of sexual intercourse when they feel especially loving towards each other. But it doesn't happen to people this way until they're grown-up – at least 17 or 18.

There are some slang words for an orgasm, and other things to do with sex, but most people think they're rude, so it's best not to say them.

ADuring an orgasm a girl feels intense pleasure in her clitoris and vagina, and a boy feels it in his penis. From the age of about 13, boys and girls can give themselves orgasms by masturbating. An orgasm is usually the climax of sexual intercourse, but grown-ups can also give each other orgasms by masturbating each other or by licking or sucking the clitoris or penis; if they do it at the same time it's called "69" because they lie head to toe. Boys and men find it much easier to have orgasms when they're enjoying sexual intercourse – it happens nearly every time, but may not for girls and women. If a couple don't want to have a baby, masturbating each other or having oral sex means that sperm don't go inside the vagina so the woman can't get pregnant. Two women can do these things to each other and so can two men. Anal sex is when the penis goes into the anus, and it can happen between two men or a man and a woman, so long as they are both happy about it. With any kind of sex, people have to be considerate, and be kind and gentle.

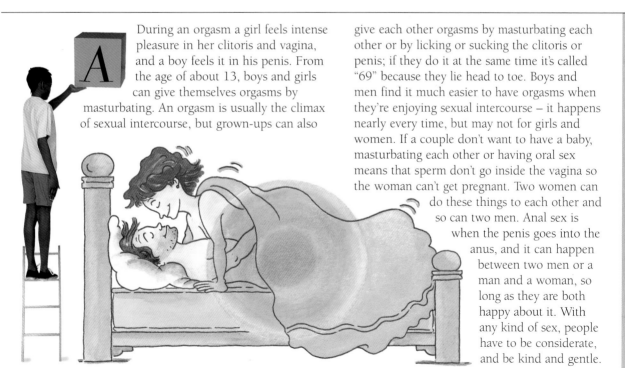

Q What does it mean if you're "gay"?

- *What is a homosexual?* • *What is a lesbian?*
- *What is a queer?* • *How can you tell if someone is gay?*
- *Why are some people gay?* • *Will I be a homosexual?*

Children have no difficulty in accepting a variety of relationships among the adults they know, but they will be naturally curious about the differences. Giving your children straightforward answers to questions about homosexual relationships, just as you would about heterosexual ones, will help to prevent prejudice or misunderstanding from taking hold right from the start.

different from anyone else, but to say that they are different is the same as saying that anyone of a different race, skin colour or religious background is somehow inferior. You can emphasize that these should never be grounds for cruel treatment or bullying.

- Pre-school children are unlikely to ask about homosexuality or what "gay" means because even if they hear the words, they are unlikely to be sensitive to the context in which the word was used.
- There is no need to go into detail about male homosexual practices with children under eight years old; they have enough difficulty getting to grips with the mechanics of heterosexual sex and reproduction. But when discussing homosexual relationships, remember to put the same emphasis on love, respect and emotions as you would in any discussion about sex.

WHAT ELSE TO KNOW

We have no way of knowing who will be homosexual (loving the same gender as oneself) or heterosexual (loving the opposite gender), and one of your children could easily turn out to be homosexual. If you yourself judge gays to be abnormal, your child will be afraid ever to come to you again with sensitive subjects, particularly if she turns out to have homosexual preferences from quite an early age, as many homosexuals have said they do. Your child may get into all sorts of trouble because she has lost confidence in you, and will try to deal with problems without your help. You will in effect be instrumental in losing your child.

WHAT'S BEHIND THIS QUESTION

There's probably nothing out of the way behind questions of this sort. Your child is fact-finding, just as if she were asking, "What's an optician ...an accountant... a sprinter?". Do find out however if your child has heard the word used in a pejorative way or as the butt of jokes. This is almost certainly the case if your child asks you the meaning of one of the slang words for a homosexual, and you'll have to correct the prejudice that your child has unwittingly acquired.

GUIDELINES FOR YOUR ANSWERS

- Ask your child where she first came across the word because this is an excellent opportunity to teach your child tolerance. You can say that homosexuals are no

Other things you may be asked...

- *What's a fag or a poof?*
- *Are they born like that?*
- *Do gay people have sex?*
- *Do gays get married?*
- *Can gay people have children?*

See also *What is sex? p. 18* • *What's a contraceptive? p. 30* • *What is AIDS? p. 92*

Children under six are not likely to ask questions about homosexuality, because close friendships between the same sex are not noteworthy, and they are not aware of different adults' sexual orientation. If a mature 5–6 year old raises the subject, adapt my answer for the 6–8 age band, below.

A A gay person likes people of the same sex, or gender, so a gay man is attracted to men and a gay woman – a lesbian – prefers other women, and they can have sex together if they love each other. "Gay" is another way of describing someone who is homosexual – which is the word for someone who falls in love with other people of the same gender. The "homo" part of of the word "homosexual" means "the same". People who fall in love with someone of the opposite sex are called heterosexuals, because the "hetero" bit of the word comes from the Greek word for different. Some slang words, like "bent", "poof", "queer" or "fag", are used for male homosexuals, but they aren't good words to use. There aren't many slang words for lesbians. Loving someone of the same sex is no different from loving someone of the opposite sex. It's all love in the end, and everyone needs that.

A We don't yet know why some people are homosexual and some aren't. Two homosexual women (lesbians) or two gay men can have sex together if they love one another. Gay men make love by kissing and cuddling and masturbating each other by touching each others' penises, or one putting his penis in the other man's anus. Lesbians kiss and cuddle and masturbate each other. They can't usually have children of their own, but some lesbian women do have babies with a heterosexual man as the father. Some people like both men and women (they're called bi-sexual) and can become parents by having a relationship with the opposite sex. I don't know if you'll be gay or not, but it wouldn't matter if you were, I'll love you just the same. Gays need their families and friends to be kind and loving to them just like anyone else. Some ignorant people think they're bad – they call them names like "queer" or "poof"; they're wrong and you shouldn't use those words.

QUESTIONS ABOUT

What are
ghosts?

Are any
spirits
kind?

What
does dead
mean?

When
will I
die?

Is God
a man
or a
woman?

Why do
some
unborn
babies die?

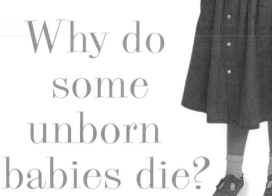

DEATH AND BEREAVEMENT • MISCARRIAGE • STILLBIRTH

THE UNKNOWN

Questions about difficult subjects like death or the existence of God pose a dilemma for parents, particularly if you do not yourselves hold firm religious beliefs. But try not to steer away from these subjects when they come up. If you are a believer, your own faith will obviously be reflected in your answers. But there are other points of view that your children will experience – so try to foster tolerance and underline the right of other people to hold different views. On the whole, it is more worrying for a child if you side-step questions about the existence of ghosts or monsters, because their imaginations will then start working overtime and provide them with explanations that are probably far more frightening than the actual truth. It is far better to be as honest and factual as possible, while at the same time being sensitive to your children's fears. Remember that your children's questions are never frivolous, so don't laugh at them or make light of them. Take them seriously, but don't dwell on them. Answer questions and worries immediately and then try to steer your child to a more positive train of thought or activity.

What is God?

Where does God live?

Q What happens when you die?

- *Why do people and animals die?* ● *What does dead mean?*
- *Do I have to die?* ● *Where do people go when they die?*
- *How do you know if someone's dead?* ● *When will I die?*

Most children are sensitive to the subject of death, if only because we talk of it in hushed tones. But this can lead to confusion and anxiety, so it is not helpful either to your children or yourselves as parents to avoid questions on the subject; dealing with them as openly as you can is a way of helping the whole family cope with a bereavement.

—— WHAT'S BEHIND THIS QUESTION ——

Young children can't conceive of life coming to an end; even a hint of this eventuality stimulates not only a rush of questions, mainly about themselves and the ones they turn to for love and care, but also terror lest their own lives be snuffed out or that they find themselves without one of their family. Children often count as family anyone they see regularly, not just their relatives. I remember my three- and five-year-old sons listing their "family" as: "Mum, Dad, Grandma, Grandpa, you, me, Ollie and Barney (their brothers), Hazie (an aunt), Oona and Slater (cousins who visited weekly), Frank (an uncle who lived with us), Mary (our cleaner), Alfie and Beaux (the dogs), Cinnamon (the cat), Alain (the gardener), Jacky (our secretary), Bob (the laundryman)", and so on. A child could be concerned and anxious if anyone in their extended "family" were ill or injured.

—— GUIDELINES FOR YOUR ANSWERS ——

● You should try to be clear about the subject of death right from the start. Never use euphemisms such as, "Granny has just gone to sleep." It could make your child afraid of going to sleep and could result in troublesome bedtimes and nightmares. Neither should you say, "Grandpa's gone away." Your child will lose her trust in you when Grandpa doesn't come back.
● Use religious explanations according to your beliefs, but be prepared for demonstrations of childhood logic like, "If God loves us why did he let our baby die?"

● Be truthful but try to keep your own emotions in check, because you may frighten your child. It doesn't mean, however, that you should not share your grief if you are particularly upset by a bereavement. Let your child know why you are tearful – explain that you miss the person who has died very much at the moment, but stress the positive memories you have of that person.
● Use examples from a child's experience to explain death. For instance, talk about a baby bird that has died because it fell out of a nest, or a pet animal dying, or even leaves dying in the autumn. This is a way of showing that all things die, and that it's natural. Check that your child understands the answer and repeat if necessary.
● If a pet dies, most pre-school children will simply be curious to find out what has happened to the animal and a short answer will be enough.

—— WHAT ELSE TO KNOW ——

Your child may not be able to cope with philosophy or faith, so keep your explanations very simple when you portray death in religious terms, otherwise your child will be more mystified than ever. Don't portray death as painful, that's very frightening.

Other things you may be asked...

- *Did he die because he'd been bad?*
- *What's a funeral/cremation?*
- *What happens to them in the coffin?*
- *Do people wake up after they've died?*
- *What will I do if you die?*

See also *Why do some babies die? p. 42* ● *What is God? p. 44* ● *What is AIDS? p. 92*

A "Dead" means a person or animal stops breathing and their body doesn't work any more. Usually people and animals only die when they have grown very old.

FOR AGES 2–4

A Something that dies – like that dead baby bird we saw last summer – can't come back. Most people and animals don't know when they're dying. Their heart stops or they quietly stop breathing.

FOR AGES 4–6

A Nobody really knows exactly what happens when we die, but our bodies stop working: we stop breathing, the heart doesn't beat, the muscles don't work and the brain stops thinking for ever. Most people die naturally because they're very old and their bodies are worn out. Usually they don't feel pain and just gradually become unconscious and gently die. But some people die from serious illnesses or accidents. None of us knows for sure where people go after they've died but we know there's no more worry or pain and that's good. I'm very unlikely to die until I'm much, much older so you needn't worry about it, because by then you'll be grown up.

FOR AGES 6–8

A You will die one day, everybody does, but it's such a long way off that you don't need to think about it. But dying is natural and although we're sad to lose someone we love very much, we must be prepared for older people like Granny and Grandpa to die one day. We won't forget them and all the good things we did together. No one dies as a punishment unless a court says so. When people die, their bodies are put in a box called a coffin, which may be buried in a grave. No one wakes up in a coffin because a doctor tests that a person really is dead before he or she is put in it. Other people prefer to be cremated – burned – and their ashes are kept at the crematorium or spread on the ground where they used to be very happy. A funeral is when a dead person is buried or cremated. People can say a final goodbye and share the good memories of when the person was alive.

FOR AGES 8–11

Q Why do some babies die?

- *What is a miscarriage?* ● *What is a stillbirth?*
- *What's an abortion?* ● *If you fall down will the baby die?*
- *Is it worse for the baby to die before or after it's born?*

The loss of a baby through miscarriage or stillbirth is a tragedy for the parents, but it can be difficult for other children in the family to understand the grief felt for an entity they haven't had time to get to know. Providing factual answers to questions from your children can allay their fears and help you to cope with grief.

WHAT'S BEHIND THIS QUESTION

All children, irrespective of age, are interested in what happened to them when they were babies, even in events long before they were born. They're also interested in what could have happened to them when they were younger. Your child probably won't ask this question unless he has heard about a miscarriage or stillbirth. If you have told your child that you are expecting another baby, or if you or someone close to you has the misfortune to lose a baby through miscarriage, stillbirth or prematurity, the questions will stem from feelings of anxiety about the same thing happening again. Older children may have heard something about abortion, and the question should be answered honestly.

GUIDELINES FOR YOUR ANSWERS

- Take your child's questions seriously, but be reassuring – he is probably frightened. You might ask, "Are you afraid of anything?" before you start.
- Your child will need lots of encouragement to believe that stillbirth and neonatal death is so rare that it isn't necessary to worry about it.
- It is also helpful to tell children that babies who miscarry are often "weak" and probably wouldn't have lived very long anyway.

- If you, personally, have miscarried, emphasize that what you want is another really lovely, healthy child like him and that it doesn't mean any future pregnancy will also end in miscarriage.
- Use any experience of death which your child may already have had – among family or close friends – to explain that you can say goodbye in the same positive way to a baby who is stillborn or dies soon after birth.

WHAT ELSE TO KNOW

Some statistics might help you as background to your answers. It is said that a third of all first pregnancies miscarry in the first eight weeks, and many women do not even realize they are pregnant when it happens. There are many reasons why miscarriages occur, but the two main reasons for early miscarriages are:

- That the baby would be abnormal in some way; it's nature's way of dealing with seriously damaged offspring.
- That the uterus is in some way immature, which means it would not be strong enough to carry the baby to term. The uterus may need a trial run before it's ready for pregnancy.

Other things you may be asked...

- *Does a baby ever die in its Mummy's tummy?*
- *Will you die if the baby dies?*
- *Does it hurt the baby when it dies?*
- *How does the baby get out if it's dead?*
- *How do you know the baby's died?*

See also *Where did I come from? p. 12* ● *Does the baby grow inside you? p. 14* ● *How does the baby get out? p. 16*

A Some babies are too weak to grow properly, so they die. It doesn't happen very often, and most babies grow up to be big and strong like you.

A Some unborn babies never grow properly and die when they're tiny, then slip out through their Mummies' vaginas. Sometimes a baby dies just after it's born, especially if it is born before it's ready. The baby's Mummy is all right, although she'll be very sad.

A "miscarriage" means that for some reason a baby dies in its Mummy's tummy and the pregnancy ends long before the baby is ready to be born. It's very rare for a baby to die after it's born unless it has something really wrong with its heart or lungs or blood, or it was born much too early. It's better for a mother and baby if the unborn baby dies when it is still very tiny. Then the mother may not even feel when it happens. But if it's bigger a mother nearly always knows because the baby stops kicking. Our baby is still kicking – feel it! Healthy babies, like you were, are so firmly fixed that nothing will shift them until they're ready to be born – not even falling down the stairs!

A When unborn babies die it is usually because they aren't properly formed. If they are seriously abnormal, like having no heart or no brain, they die very soon, usually in the first three months of pregnancy. If a baby dies later on in pregnancy, it may be because the placenta, which helps to feed the baby and give it oxygen, isn't working very well or because the mother is very ill. The words "miscarriage" and "abortion" mean the same thing. When a baby dies in pregnancy and the mother loses it, it's called a "spontaneous abortion", which means it happens by itself. If for some reason a pregnancy has to be stopped by doctors it is also called an abortion. People usually use the word "miscarriage" for a baby that dies from natural causes, and the word "abortion" for a pregnancy that is stopped on purpose. An early miscarriage doesn't cause pain to the baby and not usually to the mother; the tiny baby slips out like a menstrual period. But when the baby is more than 7cm (3in) long you can see it and the parents are very upset. If a baby who grows through pregnancy dies just before or at the birth, it is called a "stillbirth". The baby probably doesn't feel pain. A stillbirth is very sad; the baby is named and there is a funeral and people grieve for the baby like we did when Grandpa died. But stillbirths are rare: they only happen if something is badly wrong.

● *What happens when you die? p. 40*

Q What is God?

- *Who is God?* - *Is God a man or a woman?*

- *Do you believe in God?* - *Where does God live?*

- *Did God make the world/me?* - *Is God black or white?*

Whether or not you as parents are believers, at some stage your child is likely to ask pointed and searching questions about the nature of God. It is a good idea to think through for yourself what your answers are likely to be. Children can be surprisingly profound in their thinking because they come to subjects like this with open minds.

WHAT'S BEHIND THIS QUESTION

These are the sorts of questions a child being brought up in a basically Judaeo-Christian background might ask, whether or not you as a family practise a particular religion. In most Western countries with a Judaeo-Christian historical tradition the whole culture is permeated with imagery that children will notice, including the idea of a single all-powerful being called "God". Your young child won't be asking questions about faith – it's a concept most children can't grasp till the age of seven or eight when they begin to understand other complicated concepts like justice, charity and equality. But almost all children are fascinated by superhuman beings who appear to be all-knowing and all-seeing. Their questions often relate to the extent of God's omnipotence and omnipresence (they may hear someone say that "God is everywhere" or, more worryingly, that "God knows what you are doing all the time"), so they're looking for boundaries.

GUIDELINES FOR YOUR ANSWERS

- Humanizing God (as opposed to Jesus) is not necessarily a good idea because it can lead to intolerance of other religions' concepts of God. The idea of God is a difficult one to put over simply and in an unbiased way.

- If you're a believer, you naturally want your child to think the way that you do; and vice versa if you are a non-believer. Faith in something is essential for most people's happiness and equilibrium but try not to be too hard on your child if she has doubts or lacks enthusiasm. As your children get older help them to make up their own minds about it. If they see religion as something inflexible and intolerant, it could make them hostile to you and eventually may lead them to throw out all faith – including faith in you.

- A healthy spiritual life is something all children can benefit from, as long as it is not used blindly to justify political or even military actions.

- Teach your child that people who believe in God generally see Him as a force for good and love. Most religions acknowledge that human beings are imperfect; in fact many religions are based on a human need to attain some sort of perfection through God. Where you can, relate faith – yours or other people's – to the world we live in and the reality of people's behaviour.

WHAT ELSE TO KNOW

- You will probably want to answer these questions according to your own beliefs. However, although I have written some from a Christian standpoint, I have also tried to show the range of beliefs about the nature of God from a non-Christian perspective.

- Even if you're a non-believer, you still need to explain what is meant by "God". Remember your children will eventually make up their own minds about spirituality and you should encourage them to do so.

Other things you may be asked...

- *What's a worshipper?*
- *What's a believer?*
- *Can you ever see God?*
- *Why do my friends have different Gods from me?*

See also *What happens when you die? p. 40* - *What is religion? p. 46*

FOR AGES 2-4

A God is love. When I say, "I love you", that's God. God makes us love people and animals, and helps us to see all the things that are beautiful in the world, whether it's all the stars in the sky or tiny flowers in the grass.

FOR AGES 4-6

A Every time we want to do something good, that's God; every time we feel love, that's God. Everybody feels love for something, sometime, and God is that feeling. You can't see God but because lots of people feel love, love is everywhere and so is God. Some people believe that God started the world, and there are different stories of how God made all the plants, animals and people.

FOR AGES 6-8

A God isn't a man or a woman and God isn't black or white, because God isn't a person. God doesn't have a house like ours, because God is everywhere, and in everything. God is like a very good and powerful spirit. People started to think about God thousands of years ago. Some people believe there are lots of Gods, but the Jews were the first people to believe in just one God for everybody. Jesus was a Jew whom Christians believe to be God in the form of a man. People say God is in heaven, but that isn't a place in the sky – heaven is a way to describe the special feeling of goodness some people believe they will find with God after they have died.

FOR AGES 8-11

A Thousands of years ago, people who lived in different places each developed a different idea of God or lots of Gods, so there are many Gods and different ways of worshipping. Most Christians believe that Jesus really was God in the form of a man and that there is no difference between God the Father and God the Son – but that by becoming man and suffering in the same way as lots of people do in the world, God would show how much he loved everybody. Some people also believe that there's a force for evil in the world, which has been given various names such as the Devil, who is said to live in a place called hell. But as the Devil is not a person, no one can say for sure what hell really is. People who believe in a God are "believers"; those who don't are "non-believers" or atheists, and those who aren't sure are called "agnostics".

Nigerian ancestor god

Jesus Christ

Buddha

Osiris, Egyptian god

Ganesha, Hindu God of wisdom

Q What is religion?

- *Why are there so many religions?* ● *Which religion is right?*
- *Why do people from different religions fight each other?*
- *Why do people from different religions wear special clothes?*

Answering questions about other religions positively will help your children to be tolerant as well as broaden their view beyond the immediate environment of home and school. Help your children by pointing out the similarities within the different traditions, through examples like the various creation myths and stories.

WHAT'S BEHIND THIS QUESTION

These questions indicate that your child has discovered that there are different religions and traditions from those of your family. Most younger children will ask questions because they are genuinely curious; just as they want to know why there are basic differences between boys and girls, they also want to know why their friends may lead different lives and believe different things. However, if the questions imply that they have picked up concepts of "better/worse" and "superior/inferior" – and older children may have received this from other children or their families – then you should be careful to prevent such an outlook developing in your child; religious intolerance is often associated with racism and bullying.

GUIDELINES FOR YOUR ANSWERS

- Questions about religious beliefs provide you with an opportunity to teach your child tolerance and love of humanity, which is common to most religious faiths.
- Try your best to teach comparative religion. Even if you do not agree with the beliefs of a different religion, you can still acknowledge others' right to worship as they will; different religions should not be in competition.

- Of course it's natural to bring your children up initially in your own faith, but make it clear that when they are older and able to think it through properly for themselves, they will be free to choose whichever faith they wish and that they'll be just as welcome.
- Squash anything that resembles racist thinking or bullyboy tactics. Teach equality and fairness.

WHAT ELSE TO KNOW

- Children will note the difference in colour of someone's skin or in the way they worship, but they don't think of it as a mark of superiority or inferiority. It's us adults who them teach that.
- Left to themselves, children of all nationalities and beliefs play together and get on very well. It is adults who introduce bias and prejudice.
- Develop your child's innate sense of fairness and build on her unprejudiced view of the world and people. If she shows interest in other religions, ask her, "What do you think?"

People pray in many ways
Everyone should be free to worship in their own way.

Other things you may be asked...

- *Are all religions just as good?*
- *Are you friends with people from other religions?*
- *Does our God take care of people from other religions?*
- *Why do they go to church/temple on a different day?*
- *Do all religions believe in a God?*

See also *Why isn't my skin brown? p. 68* ● *What happens when you die? p. 40* ● *What is God? p. 44*

A Because people come from places all over the world, they do different things and live different lives. And they also believe in different Gods: for instance Christians believe in Christ and Hindus have Vishnu.

A When people follow special rules about what kind of God they believe in, it's called religion. People of the same religion pray to their God in special places like churches, temples or mosques, and sometimes they have to wear particular clothes or have their hair in a special way. In our religion we believe that God loves everyone including people who don't worship Him in the same way.

A Different peoples around the world have made their own Gods and written about them in their own books. People who believe in the same God set out their way of worshipping; this is what's called a religion. Most religions have one day of the week set aside for worship as well as special festivals such as Christmas, Ramadan, or Diwali. We have lots of friends who belong to other religions – David and Margot are Jewish, Jill and Bob are Buddhists, and Yindi and Nabeel follow the Islamic faith. People believe that their religion will help them to lead better lives.

A Sometimes the believers of a particular religion thought everyone else should believe it so they tried to convert them. They even thought people were wicked if they didn't follow the same religion so they punished them or went to war against them. Some people still see others who believe in different religions as their enemies, even if they are not interested in trying to convert them. But everyone should be free to follow a religion and worship their God without being troubled, because it's a private matter for you alone to decide. You can still be a good person without believing in God at all, or belonging to any particular religion. You can decide later when you've had time to think about it. We'll still love you, whatever you decide.

Shinto shrine

Islamic mosque

Christian church

Buddhist temple

Q Will I be safe in the dark?

- *Can I sleep with the light on?* • *What are ghosts?*
- *Will a monster hide in my room in the dark?*
- *How do I know nasty things won't come?*

Irrational fears are not exclusive to childhood, of course, but children are particularly prone to them as they try to make sense of new experiences. Small children with vivid imaginations may turn apparently banal or even happy images into objects of fear, and their fears need to be handled sensitively to avoid long-term problems.

WHAT'S BEHIND THIS QUESTION

It's very easy to imagine all kinds of horrors in the dark, as we all know, and adulthood doesn't necessarily bring immunity from fantastical fears. So it's not surprising that some children are frightened of the dark, of monsters, witches, dragons and creepy crawlies. Children have active imaginations, and as far as they are concerned all these things are real because fantasy is difficult to separate from reality. Shadows on the wall, creaks on the stairs only seem to convince your child that his worst fears are confirmed. Be alert to frightening TV programmes and films, and the more gruesome fairy stories, which may quite unexpectedly trigger some irrational fear. Even clowns or pantomime characters can disturb the susceptible child.

GUIDELINES FOR YOUR ANSWERS

- It's intelligent to be afraid of the dark, it's not silly or wimpish, so never make fun of a fearful child.
- Help your child to overcome his fears by finding out what you can do to be reassuring. It may be a safe night-light in the bedroom, or a light left on in the hall, or you could stay with your child occasionally until he's

asleep. Be prepared to do any of these things so that your child feels secure enough to go to sleep unafraid, and therefore doesn't have nightmares or night terrors.

- If you find your child has been watching a frightening TV programme and you haven't been able to prevent it, you can help to avoid nightmares if you bring your child back into the real world by doing something mundane like teeth cleaning, hair brushing, planning tomorrow's sports kit. Or you can talk positively about something really good that happened, or anticipate an exciting and happy event, like a birthday party or a holiday. Once they were over the age of nine, and after the usual "good nights", all my children went to sleep listening to their own choice in music, which prevented frightening thoughts.
- Reassure your child as he goes to sleep by keeping up a running commentary from another room. Use a calm, quiet voice, but make sure he can hear you.

WHAT ELSE TO KNOW

- Many frightening memories emanate from images or fantasies in the dark. Your child can't verbalize them and you'll never know what they are. Simply respect your child's fears and be sympathetic, consoling and reassuring at all times.
- Help your child get over a shock by letting him go to sleep while lying next to you downstairs, or starting the night in your bed. He can go back to his own room when he's more confident. Try switching the furniture around in his bedroom so it looks and feels different.

Other things you may be asked...

- *Are those monsters on that TV programme really there?*
- *Are any spirits kind?*
- *How will I know there's no one outside my room?*
- *Can monsters hurt me?*
- *Is there someone in the cupboard?*

See also *What happens when you die? p. 40* • *What does violence mean? p. 84*

A You can have a night-light in your room or I'll leave the light on outside. Don't worry, no one will harm you – Daddy and Mummy are here. I'll keep talking to you for a while outside the room so you know I'm here. Just call "Good night Mummy and Daddy", and we'll say "Good night" back.

A Things like ghosts, witches and monsters aren't real – they're just make-believe in stories, but even in stories they aren't always bad. But because they aren't real, they can't come in the dark. If you don't believe in ghosts and monsters they can't hurt you, can they? But if you're worried, we'll get Alfie to lie outside your door and he'll keep you safe, because he always barks if he hears something.

A There's no one in your cupboard, let's go and look. There's nothing there at all, so we'll shut the door together so now we both know that no-one could possibly get in. And we'll look under the bed and behind the curtains just to make you feel better. We won't be far away – we'll be in the living room, don't worry. But just this once you can keep your reading light on for a while. Let's find a book with a happy story. Put your books away at 8.30 and I'll leave the light on outside. You can listen to some music, nice and quietly, as you go to sleep. I'll pop in to check that you're all right before I go to bed.

A That was a nasty dream you had – but it wasn't real – it was only a dream. I expect it was just because you watched that film about the dinosaurs. Well, you know that was just a story – with actors and special effects – the dinosaurs looked real but they weren't really. We could get a book out of the library that explains how it's done.

Why don't I lie on the bed before you go back to sleep and we'll talk about some good times you've had when you really enjoyed yourself, like when we went to the fun fair. What was your best ride? Do you remember the sun was shining and the sky was blue and the banners were waving, and from the top of the Ferris wheel we could see right over to the other side of the park, and you had the money for an ice cream in your pocket.

QUESTIONS ABOUT

Can I miss
school
for once?

Where's
Mum
gone?

Is it my
fault?

Why do
I always
get the
blame?

Am I
adopted?

Why can't
Daddy live
with us?

● SEPARATION ● DIVORCE ● STEP-PARENTING ● ADOPTION ●

RELATIONSHIPS

A child's world revolves round close personal relationships, first at home with parents and siblings and then at school with friends and teachers. Changes, upsets or arguments with any of these people can have a profound effect on a child, in ways that may be difficult

How can I make friends?

for him to articulate. Although in all probability your child's questions are very straightforward, be alert to the possible scenarios behind them. At first sight, the questions may not appear to relate directly to the problem or uncertainty that is really bothering him, and you may need to probe gently to get to the bottom of it. But if you suspect anything untoward, try to discover the real reason for your child's concern without provoking antagonism or feelings of guilt. These can be damaging to a child perhaps coming to terms with the emotional turmoil of a break-up, so try to clarify your child's anxieties and give straightforward answers. The questions here are united by a threat to your child's security, even though the circumstances may differ, so when your six-year-old daughter falls out with her

What's divorce?

inseparable best friend, she may be as devastated as another child who has to cope with his parents' divorce. It is all a question of degree, but what is important is that your love and reassurance provide the cornerstone to your answers.

SIBLINGS ● FRIENDSHIPS ● PROBLEMS AT SCHOOL

Q Where's Daddy/Mummy gone?

- *Doesn't Mummy/Daddy love you any more?*
- *Why do you and Mummy/Daddy fight?*
- *Why does Mummy/Daddy sleep in the spare room now?*

Trying to protect children caught in the middle of the breakdown of their parents' relationship can be heartbreaking for both mother and father. However, being as honest as you can when you answer their questions is one way to help them feel secure about your love for them, in spite of what is happening between you as a couple. Try not to badmouth a partner, no matter what your personal feelings may be – that person is still your child's other parent.

WHAT'S BEHIND THIS QUESTION

Problems arise in all relationships; in learning that Mum and Dad may not always be the best of friends, your child is learning a lesson about life. He is fine as long as he is confident of your mutual love, but when he first realizes you are getting on badly with each other he may feel that his whole world is breaking up and that he can't trust anyone if he cannot rely on his parents. Children in this situation become insecure, may regress to infantile behaviour, become naughty and attention-seeking for reassurance, and nearly always blame themselves for what's happened.

GUIDELINES FOR YOUR ANSWERS

- If you fall out with your partner, reassure your child that even though you disagree, you still love him no matter what happens. And if you manage to patch things up, include your child in the reconciliation so that everyone in the family can feel united.

- Whether or not there is a permanent breakdown of relations, it's essential that children feel secure about their future, so reassure them that they will be safe even if their mother or father has gone.
- Children often worry about things that never occur to us, like who will take them to school. Always ask what's worrying them, always tell the truth in a way they can understand and once they're old enough, warn them about what's going to happen – don't spring things on them at the last minute.
- The answers here are from the point of view of a mother who is separating from her partner; if necessary, adjust your answers to suit your situation .

WHAT ELSE TO KNOW

- Your child will soak up emotional signals; if you're sad, the chances are he will be too.
- Children want to be told about break-ups; if they're kept in the dark, they stop trusting and respecting you.
- Don't think your child won't know what's going on, or try to shield him from it. Children feel insecure if they only know part of the story.
- If you move out, you must tell your child that you're not taking your love with you and that you'll write and visit often. If possible, give him a specific date to look forward to and never let him down.
- By continuing to visit regularly and helping to maintain a child's routine, grandparents, other family members and close friends can be wonderful in reassuring a child that his family still exists and loves him.

Other things you may be asked...

- *Why are you shouting at each other?*
- *Does that mean Mummy/Daddy doesn't love me any more?*
- *Why do people stop loving each other?*
- *Is it my fault?*
- *Will Mummy/Daddy come back?*

See also *What's divorce? p. 54* • *Do I have to call him Daddy? p. 56*

FOR AGES 2–4

A Mummy and Daddy are cross with each other, so Mummy may decide to go away and live somewhere else for a while. Mummy's really sorry she won't be with you but we both still love you very much and always will. Mummy will come and see you as often as possible – at least once a week.

FOR AGES 4–6

A Mummy and Daddy are cross with each other at the moment and it's difficult to sleep with someone if you're angry with them. Mummies and Daddies don't always stay together for ever. Sometimes they find they don't love each other any more. It's going to be difficult for Mummy to leave you because she still loves you, but she'll come back to see you every week. Remember, it's not your fault.

FOR AGES 6–8

A Mummy and Daddy are separated at the moment. We disagree about things and we don't like being cross with each other all the time, specially as we know it upsets you. We're going to try and work things out so we can live together again, but we may not be able to. Even though we're trying very hard, we could find we don't love each other any more and don't want to live together. Mummy hasn't stopped loving you, and it isn't your fault – you're not to blame. She hasn't gone because you've been bad. I'll be here to look after you and Mummy will visit you every week.

FOR AGES 8–11

A Mum and I have done everything we can to stay together, I promise. We don't want to upset our children and we wish we could still be happy together but we can't be. Mum and I don't love each other any more and Mum has the right to see if she can find someone else to love. She'll always love you and write to you, visit you and go on holiday with you. Nothing you did has made her go – you are not to blame in any way. She just had to go for herself. We're still married at the moment, even though we aren't living together, but one day we may get divorced. That means we won't be married to each other any more, but we'll never stop being your Mum and Dad. We might still do things together, like going to the cinema and having a meal afterwards.

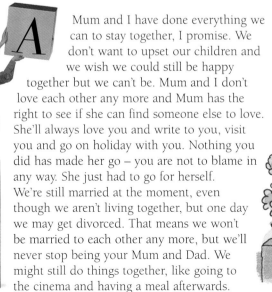

Q What's divorce?

- *Why are you and Daddy getting divorced?*
- *Why can't we still be together?* • *Do you have to get divorced?*
- *Was Daddy bad to you?* • *Will I still be able to see Daddy?*

Divorce is never easy for a couple, but when there are children involved it is much harder for all concerned. Whatever the circumstances of a divorce, children need to be reassured that their needs will be met, that they are in no way to blame for the breakdown of their parents' marriage and that both their parents will continue to love them as before.

WHAT'S BEHIND THIS QUESTION

Doubt is one of the worst feelings for a child, leading to fear and confusion, so never leave your child in any doubt that you both love her and, whatever happens, your child will continue to be looked after at home by one of you. It's very revealing talking to children whose parents have been through a divorce; children always want to know that they are not to blame, that they're still loved by both parents and, if possible, that their parents will remain – and act like– friends. When asked about our divorce, one of my sons said, "It was okay, Mum, I could handle it because you and Dad were obviously still friends." For this section, the questions are answered from the point of view of a mother who has care of the children, with the father absent. As before, adjust the answers to your own circumstances.

GUIDELINES FOR YOUR ANSWERS

- Children under five perceive the world in relation to themselves, so it's best to explain at least partially what's going on, even at this young age. If you don't, children will invent their own explanations, mistakenly blaming themselves for causing problems in the family.

- If you don't give a plausible explanation of why you and your partner are divorcing, your child may come up with her own wild explanations, such as, "Mummy left because I don't keep my room tidy" or, "Daddy was upset because I wet the bed/I am clumsy/can't do my sums/lost my pocket money".
- Feelings of guilt are damaging for a child already coming to terms with the insecurity that a break-up can trigger. Ask questions to clarify your child's anxieties, and give simple straightforward answers.
- Whatever the circumstances of your divorce, and no matter how bitter you may feel, try not to transmit these feelings to your child. Your child is half of each partner and will feel worthless if you show your dislike for the other person who made her.

WHAT ELSE TO KNOW

- If you are left as a single parent, try not to be upset when your child misses her absent parent, and avoid pretending that he or she doesn't exist.
- Tell your child's teachers what's happened and ask them to keep a close eye on her to avoid difficulties at school. Give your child space to voice worries; listen and take them seriously.
- Older children may worry about having enough money. Divorce does put a strain on many families' finances, but try not to burden your child with it, as it could provide another reason for her to feel guilty.

Other things you may be asked...

- *Do you and Daddy still love me?*
- *Will Daddy still love me when you're divorced?*
- *Will I still be able to see Grandma and Grandpa?*
- *Will I still go to the same school?*

See also *Do I have to call him Daddy? p. 56* • *Where's Daddy/Mummy gone? p. 52*

A divorce is when two people who are married stop being married to each other because they don't love each other any more. We're getting divorced but we still love you very much and we'll take care of you just the same.

Mummy and Daddy are getting divorced because they really can't work things out to stay together. We'll do our best to be friends as that's best for all of us. Mummy and Daddy will always love you and look after you. I know you love us both and you'll be able to have time with each of us, I promise. Daddy will have a different home but even if you don't see him every day he'll still love you.

Divorce is sad. Nobody wants to split up a family; that's why I cry now and then. We would still like the family to stay together but Daddy feels he needs to make a fresh start. Divorce is hard and sometimes we are unkind to each other, but you're not to blame for anything, it's not your fault. Husbands and wives can stop loving each other; they change during marriage, especially if they were quite young when they got married. But we'll never stop loving you – we both love you very much. We'll arrange for you to see Daddy often and to spend holidays with him. You'll help us both if you tell him you love him. And you will be able to see Grandpa just as often as before.

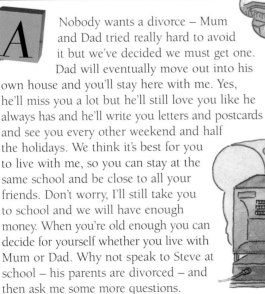

Nobody wants a divorce – Mum and Dad tried really hard to avoid it but we've decided we must get one. Dad will eventually move out into his own house and you'll stay here with me. Yes, he'll miss you a lot but he'll still love you like he always has and he'll write you letters and postcards and see you every other weekend and half the holidays. We think it's best for you to live with me, so you can stay at the same school and be close to all your friends. Don't worry, I'll still take you to school and we will have enough money. When you're old enough you can decide for yourself whether you live with Mum or Dad. Why not speak to Steve at school – his parents are divorced – and then ask me some more questions.

Q Do I have to call him Daddy?

● *Do you love me as much as Sarah and Tim?*

● *Have I got two Mummies/two Daddies?*

● *Why can't Daddy still live with us?*

If you are a single parent who has started a relationship, it is painful if your child finds it difficult to accept your new partner. However, it's natural, so everyone involved needs to be patient, understanding and willing to compromise in the task of winning the trust of your child.

WHAT'S BEHIND THIS QUESTION

Nothing can dislodge the central role that parents play in a child's life, so when a child is confronted by a prospective step-parent, confusion and unhappiness can be the result. A child may become very insecure, mistrustful of all adults and need a lot of reassurance. A child's anxiety at losing the estranged parent completely can be intense, particularly if he feels that the new step-parent is going to usurp the natural parent's position – the classic fairy tale scenario. All aspects of the life of a child in this situation may be affected: he may stop eating, start having nightmares, become naughty and do badly at school. If there are stepbrothers and sisters, or a new baby is on the way, your child may worry that you will withdraw your love and transfer it to the new members of the family.

GUIDELINES FOR YOUR ANSWERS

● When you take on a new partner in a long-term relationship, whether or not you re-marry, your main aim should be to reassure your child with words and actions that show very clearly that you still love him and always will, come what may. You may have to repeat this over and over. Tell him at least once a day how terrific he is, especially last thing at night.

● When you're introducing a step-parent to your child never run down the biological parent. Present your new partner as a bonus. It's not surprising that children have difficulty with the concept of two sets of parents. When he acquired me as a stepmother, my stepson's problems were solved when he found other friends at school who had two "Dads".

● Never talk about "Your new Mummy/Daddy" as if your child's real parent no longer exists. A younger child especially may see this as a rejection of his natural parent and may fear that it means he won't be allowed to see the absent parent.

● I have answered the questions from the point of view of a mother taking a new partner who also has children of his own. Adapt this to your own situation.

WHAT ELSE TO KNOW

● Never force the pace of acceptance, go at the child's speed. A step-parent's initial aim should be to make friends and, if closeness follows, all well and good.

● Try to minimize tension between the step-parent and absent parent. A step-parent should expect few parental rights – you can't replace the biological parent nor should you want to. I used to encourage my stepsons to see their mother when they wanted and not to conform to formal access visits. As a step-parent you don't want to be remembered for jealousy or resentment.

Other things you may be asked...

■ *Am I still allowed to see Mummy/Daddy?*

■ *Does he/she have live with us?*

■ *What's a half-sister/brother?*

■ *What's a stepsister/brother?*

See also *Where's Daddy/Mummy gone? p. 52* ● *What's divorce? p. 54* ● *Why am I adopted? p. 58*

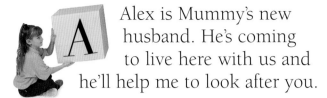

FOR AGES 2-4

Alex is Mummy's new husband. He's coming to live here with us and he'll help me to look after you. He's looking forward to getting to know you. Daddy knows all about him and you'll see Daddy just as often as you did before.

FOR AGES 4-6

A step-parent is the word for a person who marries someone who already has children. The step-parent isn't the actual Mummy or Daddy to those children but helps look after them. Both kinds of parents can love you. You don't have to call your stepfather "Daddy" – just use his first name. I love your stepfather, but your Daddy is still very special to you, and you can see him often.

FOR AGES 6-8

It's difficult to understand having two sets of Mummies or Daddies but it happens quite often. You could ask Michael and Jane at school about their stepfather. It's nice to think that there's another grown-up at home who loves you just as much as his own children. Sarah and Tim are your stepbrother and stepsister – their Mummy and Daddy are different from yours, but we love you all just the same. If Alex and I decide to have a baby, the baby would be your half-brother or sister, because it would grow in Mummy's tummy like you, but have a different father. The baby would be Tim and Sarah's half-brother or sister too, so you can share it.

FOR AGES 8-11

Your real Dad is one of the people who made you and I want you to love him and see and stay with him as often as possible, because he loves you as much as I do. Alex is your step-dad and he wants to be your friend, but he knows he can't take the place of your real Dad. We both want to make it as easy as possible for you. No matter what happens, your real Mum and Dad can't be changed and we'll always love you. We'll try to do whatever we can to make it easier for you. You can always be honest with me and tell me when you're feeling angry and upset – it's important to say how you really feel. It's hard to accept a new situation but we'll work together to make sure you're happy.

Q Why am I adopted?

- *Are you really my Mummy and Daddy?* ● *Am I adopted?*
- *Can I see my real Mummy and Daddy?*
- *How can I have two Mummies and Daddies?*

If you have adopted a child, it is important to reassure her that your love is exactly the same as the love of natural parents. Answering your child's questions honestly and making sure she knows the truth as soon as possible will help avoid the trauma of sudden discovery. Talk sensitively from the very beginning about your child being adopted so that it's accepted as normal.

WHAT'S BEHIND THIS QUESTION

The advice to the majority of parents who adopt a child when still a baby is to let your child know as early as possible, in a way that suits her age and understanding, that she is adopted. Questions will naturally arise from this early knowledge, as your child begins to link her understanding of how babies are made to her own situation. At this point she will be looking for extra reassurance that you really love her, and that you aren't going to give her away again, like her natural parents had to in the first place. If you adopt an older child who can remember her life before she came into your family, you may find the questions arise because the child wants to know why you chose *her* to adopt, rather than anyone else. Children in this situation may have an underlying insecurity that may take years to counteract. They could continue to worry that if their adopted parents get cross, they may be sent away again.

GUIDELINES FOR YOUR ANSWERS

● Like questions about sex and death, questions from your adopted child should not be shirked, because there is a danger that she may learn about the adoption from someone else, possibly even in a moment of anger. This could destroy your child's confidence in you which, as adoptive parents, you will have painstakingly built up over the years.

● Always answer a question about adoption frankly and honestly: every person has the right to know who their parents are, irrespective of age. Even if your child doesn't ask, provide the information when quite young, at three or four, in a very matter-of-fact way so that your child accepts it coolly.

● When children learn that their natural mother gave them up for adoption, they may feel worthless. You will need to demonstrate your affection in much more overt ways while they get used to the idea.

● Always praise your child's biological mother, stressing the courage she needed to give her child up for adoption, and how lucky and privileged you feel to have been able to take over as her child's parents.

WHAT ELSE TO KNOW

● Nowadays, in most countries, adults who were adopted as children can see their original birth records. This is only done on request, but if your child asks questions about her natural parents, offer to help find them when the time comes – and keep your promise.

● Tell your adopted child from your heart why you adopted her so that she will feel completely secure about your love and will grow up with self-esteem.

Other things you may be asked...

- *Will you always love me?*
- *Why did you adopt me?*
- *Why did she give me away?*
- *Will my real Mummy and Daddy love me?*
- *Will you always be my Daddy?*
- *Are you cross with me because I'm adopted?*

See also *Where did I come from? p. 12* ● *Why do I always get the blame? p. 60*

FOR AGES 2–4

Children under four years will rarely ask about adoption unless they have been recently adopted or they hear the word used. If a mature three-and-a-half year-old asks questions, base your answers on those for the 4–6 age group.

FOR AGES 4–6

A You have two Mummies and Daddies because the Daddy and Mummy who made you weren't able to look after you, which was very sad for them. So another Mummy and Daddy were found to look after you – that's us – and we think we are very lucky. Don't worry, you'll always stay with us. We love you and take care of you because now we're your Mummy and Daddy and we always will be.

FOR AGES 6–8

A If you want, I'll help you find out who your real Mummy and Daddy are when you're grown up. I believe you should try to find them. I can't say why your real Mummy gave you away, but it wasn't because she didn't love you. It was a very hard thing for her to do. I expect she'll be pleased to see you when the time comes. We adopted you because we can't make any children of our own but we know that there are lots of babies and children whose parents unfortunately aren't able to look after them. We wanted very much to give a home to one of those babies. We thought you were lovely when we first met you – and we always will.

FOR AGES 8–11

A If you want, you can find out who your real parents are when you're old enough – we'll help you to find them. I'm sure your first Mum loved you but she had to give you up for adoption because she had no choice and couldn't look after you. She probably loved you so much she wanted you to have a better life with people who could look after you and love you just as much. I feel sure she'll be very pleased to meet you when you're grown up.

I don't get cross with you just because you're adopted – I would get cross with you about things if I was your real Mum or Dad. Ask Jane – her Mum and Dad get cross with her sometimes too! We love you and want the best for you like all parents do for their children, because you really are our child.

Q Why do I always get the blame?

- *Do you love him more than me?* • *Why's she your favourite?*
- *Why's he never wrong?* • *Why am I always the naughty one?*
- *Do you wish I was more like her?*

Trying to be even-handed with all your children is one of the most difficult tasks for parents. Each child wants to feel special, and will be only too quick to show resentment if he feels that another child is being favoured by either parent.

WHAT'S BEHIND THIS QUESTION

Sibling jealousy is a reality and as some children are prone to insecurity about their parents' long-term love, they may pick up all sorts of nuances that adults give no credence to. Once they feel any hint of preference for a sibling, they will see confirmation of your favouritism in a thousand other small incidents. I would never allow an older child to be rough with a younger one, so the youngsters were always seen as protected and preferred. But that's a lesson for life – a strong aggressor can never be allowed to intimidate a weaker victim. On the other hand, a younger child might feel resentful if he has to go to bed earlier than an older sibling, or isn't allowed to see a particular TV programme which older children are watching. Very often such questions are a warning that your child is feeling left out, even unloved, and you should act quickly to reassure him in word and deed, by spending dedicated time with the aggrieved child each day and repeating all the time that you love him.

GUIDELINES FOR YOUR ANSWERS

- You can answer your child's questions with explanations, but actions will always count for more – big hugs, time spent alone with him, arranging exclusive outings, admiring a new skill, a special bedtime story.

- The main message to give is that you're fair and even-handed; though your child may perceive injustices or imbalances, it will all even out in the end. I tried to teach my four children to think in a longer timescale than one hour or one day and they learned to trust me; it might take a year but they'd all get their turn at being the special one. Children love you unconditionally: they each deserve some special attention in return.
- Stress each child's individuality – be positive about their differences, strengths and achievements.

WHAT ELSE TO KNOW

Life is not always fair. Home is the best place to learn this rather unpalatable truth. My sons were not all equally good at making friends. The outgoing, loving ones seemed to have a better time than the introspective loners. That's a fact of life, so we had to think up suitable ways to compensate each child for the discrepancies, and we didn't always get it right. Once a child was old enough, we explained our fallibility. "Life's tough" were words that were used quite often in our house.

Other things you may be asked...

- *Why does he always get the best toys?*
- *Why does she always get more sweets?*
- *Why don't you ever tell her off?*
- *Why do you let him stay off school and not me?*
- *Why is her piece always bigger than mine?*

See also *Do I have to call him Daddy? p. 56* • *Why am I adopted? p. 58* • *What's a bully? p. 82*

A We're not really cross with you all the time, it just seems that way because you remember when we are cross and forget the times when we're pleased. We think we're very lucky to have you as our little boy. After playgroup I'll take you to the park without the baby, just you and me.

A You don't always get the blame, but as you get older you learn what the naughty things are, and you can learn to stop doing them. Sara is younger than you so she doesn't know what's naughty yet. You're much bigger than her, so we probably expect you to be grown up all the time which isn't fair, especially as you do remember to be good most of the time. And we really love you very much.

A I know it's hard for you to go to bed earlier than Jennie but she is older than you and she doesn't need as much sleep. It isn't because we like her more than you, it's because you get very tired when you stay up late and then you don't enjoy yourself at school the next day and we want you to be happy and do well. Jennie's only allowed to stay up later and watch the nature programme on television because she's doing a project on it at school. During the holidays you can stay up later sometimes as well, because then you'll be able to catch up on your sleep in the morning.

A I know he's the baby so he tends to get away with things but you spoil him too, don't you? You peel his orange and give him the best bits and when he's tired you carry him on your shoulders. The baby in the family often gets spoiled by the whole family. But if you think it's really unfair, speak up and I'll do something about it. He is probably allowed to do some things at a younger age than you did but you were our first baby and we had to learn about looking after children through you; now we've learned, we may be a bit more relaxed with the younger ones. But you are the eldest and so you're very special to us, and as you're such a good older sister, I think you've earned some special privileges. You can stop sharing with Anna and we'll redecorate your room as you want it. And you can take your friends there. I have never wished you were anyone but yourself – I love you for what you are.

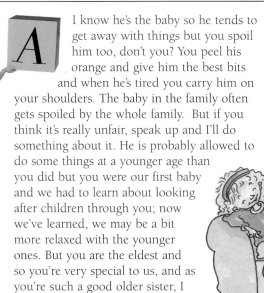

Q Why can't I make friends?

- *Why don't I have a best friend?* ● *Why doesn't anybody like me?*
- *Why does Susan tease me?* ● *Why will no one play with me?*
- *Why do they laugh at me at school?*

From school age, your child's friendships are very important to his emotional and social development. Some children naturally make lots of friends – others prefer to stick steadfastly to one particular person. Occasionally things go temporarily wrong in childhood friendships, but if your child seems to have long-term difficulty in making or keeping friends, you may have to take sensitive steps to help him.

WHAT'S BEHIND THIS QUESTION

Your child may be a natural loner and very happy to be so. Such children are often self-sufficient and independent; they have played alone happily since infancy, are easily engaged by toys, games and books and often learn to read very early. They don't need or miss friends, but once they enter the social structure of school, such children can be perceived as "different" by classmates who tend to isolate them: your child will be sensitive to that. Then there are the frequent and normal squabbles about best friends: "No, Patsy isn't YOUR best friend, she's MINE", and even four-year-olds are hurt by being shut out. Most children enjoy having friends from as early as two, but later on at school, these questions may sometimes be associated with bullying, and it is worth probing gently, using my guidelines on bullying on page 82.

GUIDELINES FOR YOUR ANSWERS

- Encourage your child's social skills from an early age by teaching him to share, to be gentle and friendly. Remember, an unloved child can't do these things.

- From the age of five many children select a favourite playmate, so try to invite different children to the house or on outings, so that he has lots to select from.
- You can't force another child to be friendly with yours, but when you invite a child to your home, involve yourself in the children's play, so that you can check that your child's responses are appropriate.
- If your child is a loner but wants friends, try giving him more responsibility to boost his confidence. Discuss with your child's teacher the possibility of giving him and a suitable partner a job, like handing out paper, as this confers status among his peers.

WHAT ELSE TO KNOW

- By the time your child is four, he can probably play with other children in an imaginative, sustained way. At this age, gender is not usually a criterion for selecting friends – and neither is race or dress, so keep your child's circle of friends mixed.
- Having an imaginary friend who is occasionally used as a scapegoat is a normal part of a younger child's development, so be patient and tolerant. By the age of seven or eight, children usually grow out of this phase and clearly know the difference between fantasy and reality. But it could be a sign of loneliness if it persists.
- From the age of six, school and peer groups can have more influence on your child than home and parents, so always consult teachers about how best to tackle problems of friendship. Together you can help your child find the best approach to making friends.

Other things you may be asked...

- *How can I have a best friend?*
- *How can I make friends?*
- *Why doesn't John want to come and play?*
- *Why doesn't anybody pick me for their team?*
- *Why can't you see my (imaginary) friend?*

See also *Why do I have to go to school? p. 64* ● *What's a bully? p. 82*

A It's nice to share things with friends. Why don't we take Barbara to see your play house, and then you can both help make tea. Tomorrow we could have John, Chris and Kate for tea as well and you can all share your toys.

A There's nothing wrong with being a bit quiet, but it doesn't mean no-one likes you. I expect there are lots of other children who prefer drawing and reading books – I know Jack does. Maybe you could ask him to go with you to the school library at lunchtime. Friends are nice, you have fun together and enjoy the same things. You don't have to have lots of friends – but we'll invite the children you like best for your birthday party.

A Mary has lots of different friends, so she probably feels a bit uncomfortable if you only want her to be best friends with you at school. Why don't you invite her over on Saturday instead so you can have lots of time together.

I've never seen your imaginary friend because she's your special invention. It's nice for you to have someone with you in your mind when you're on your own, but it's good to have your own real friends as well, so we'll have Rosie to tea, even though you say your imaginary friend doesn't like her.

A I'm sure the other children don't laugh at you because they don't like you. Perhaps they're nervous because you're often on your own. People like other people to take an interest in them, so if you let them know that you're interested in what they think and do, they'll probably be glad to make friends with you. If you hang back, they might think that you're happier on your own even though they really would like to be friends with you or pick you for their team. You need to send out the kind of message that says, "Can I join in?" But you don't have to have a lot of friends, if you don't want to. If you like, we could ask a friend to see a film or go out for a pizza, or I could tape the Sunday game, so a friend could come and watch it with you or to stay overnight at the weekend. Just think about it.

Q Why do I have to go to school?

- *Why do I have to go to playgroup/nursery school?*
- *Do I have to go to the same school as Tommy Jones?*
- *Do I have to be in Miss Smith's class?*

It's natural for younger children to be a bit reluctant about leaving the security of home and going to nursery or school, especially to start with. But parents need to be alert to problems that occur after the initial settling-in period. With older children, who have been going to school for some years, there may be deeper problems, which need to be handled sensitively.

WHAT'S BEHIND THIS QUESTION

It could be simply a grumble, a try-on, in which case you have to be firm, and talk about the good things about school, accentuating the positive aspects which your child has enjoyed in the past. A child starting nursery or full-time school for the first time is bound to need a period of adjustment, but some questions require further probing. For instance, "Can I have some more money for school?" raises the possibility of play-ground extortion, or even truancy. The former may be a sign that your child is being bullied and victimized – the latter, a sign of boredom; either way the problem needs to be dealt with. True school phobia – an irrational fear of school – is very rare but keep it at the back of your mind if your child gets ill with fear of school; you may need professional help.

GUIDELINES FOR YOUR ANSWERS

- Learning to take the rough with the smooth, to take constructive criticism, is a great basic lesson in life, and school is where your child can learn these invaluable lessons with your help, working in partnership with the staff at your children's school.

- Always be ready to listen and sympathize; let your child know that you are prepared to solve problems.
- Your child may ask you to bend school rules, or make excuses for his proposed absences: mine did. My answer was always the same: though we don't always agree with all school rules, they do serve a purpose and we keep them as best we can during school-time.
- If your child's questions reveal bullying or truancy, you should always report it to the headteacher and follow it up to make sure it is being dealt with properly by the school (see my guidelines on page 82).

WHAT ELSE TO KNOW

- Children under eight have difficulty identifying exactly what's wrong. Once my seven-year-old came home from school looking very glum; when I enquired why, he said, "The world doesn't feel right." It turned out he was worried because he couldn't learn his tables.
- If the problem stems from dislike or fear of a member of staff, talk to your child's teacher first, even if he or she is the one your child has named. A child may be transferring his nervousness about school onto that person. If there isn't any improvement after this discussion, take your worries to the headteacher.
- The arrival of a new baby may make a young child reluctant to go to school – he may feel rejected or jealous when he sees that the baby can stay at home with you. Try to organize a division of labour, so that one parent stays with the baby and the other takes the child to school so he can have a special time with you.

Other things you may be asked...

- *Why can't you always take me to school?*
- *Can I go and play with Jenny instead of going to school?*
- *Can I have more money for school?*
- *Can I miss school for once?*
- *Why can't I stay here with you and the baby?*

See also *Why can't I make friends? p. 62* • *What's a bully? p. 82*

At nursery you'll see all your friends and play with the toys we don't have at home. I'll stay with you for a little while this afternoon and then you can bring a friend home to play. You can help me choose what to have for tea.

A I can't always take you to school because I have to look after baby Maria when Daddy goes to work, but today he's going to stay with Maria, so I can take you to school and you can show me all the clever things you do there. I know school can be tiring but you learn lots of exciting new things every day. Teachers can seem a bit strict because they have so many children to look after but they're nice really.

A Going to school to learn is mostly to do with being happy and doing things you like. If you learn well, you'll be able to choose to do whatever job you want when you're older, so it's worth sticking at. You told me you'd like to be a rocket scientist – no one can become one of those if they don't learn how to write and read, and to understand numbers. I'm sure Miss Smith likes you, just like everyone else does. What's happened to make you think she might not? Are you sure she wasn't just cross about something? If there's something you don't understand we can go through it together at home and I'll have a quiet word with your teacher about it later.

A It would be better if you didn't take a day off because you'll miss something and have to make it up later. Is there something wrong at school? If you missed school today you'd miss art as well, which would be a pity, as you enjoy it. Not everyone is friendly at school and teachers don't always make lessons interesting but we have to take the rough with the smooth. Dad and Mum often work with people we don't get on with but we still have to be polite to them. Why do you want more money? Does Rob take your money? Next time he does, either tell your teacher or me straightaway and we'll do something about it.

QUESTIONS ABOUT

Why isn't my skin brown?

Will she get better?

What does racism mean?

Why is that girl's hair so curly?

Was he born like that?

RACE AND ETHNIC DIVERSITY ● PHYSICAL DISABILITY ●

DIFFERENCES

Children are not born with prejudices – they learn them. This is one of the most important things to keep in mind if your children start asking questions about racial or religious differences, disabilities or alternative ways of life, for example, vegetarianism. So the basis of your answers to all questions about differences is that everyone is the same inside, and that external differences are nothing to fear. Their questions about race or disability will present you with opportunities to teach tolerance and acceptance. Judging a person by the way they look or the food they eat is wrong – always discourage your child from thinking that way. Children have an innate sense of justice and fair play. Build on it; don't undermine or destroy it by allowing stereotypical views to take hold.

Do you eat meat?

Why is it rude to stare?

What's a vegetarian?

LEARNING DIFFICULTIES ● VEGETARIANISM ● ANIMAL WELFARE

Q Why isn't my skin brown?

- *Why is his skin a different colour from mine?*
- *Why is her hair so curly?* • *Why does Ben wear a little black cap?*
- *Why doesn't Akasi eat sausages?* • *What does racism mean?*

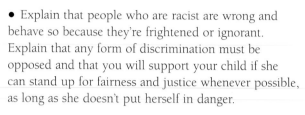

Racial prejudice in children is always the result of attitudes picked up at home or among their peer group – without these outside influences, children are not prejudiced. That isn't to say they don't notice differences; when they ask questions about their observations it is important not to overreact; as ever, honest, factual answers are the key.

WHAT'S BEHIND THIS QUESTION

Children don't worry about racial differences manifested by dress or skin colour until they are programmed to by adults. Watch a mixed group of four- to five-year-olds playing and you'll see quite clearly that they regard each other as equals. Questions about racial differences may occur innocently from simple comparison, but your child could start asking questions because she has heard others – children as well as adults – making racist remarks about people from ethnic backgrounds different from your own. This is a danger signal and needs to be treated accordingly. However, older, thoughtful children may also pick up on problems caused by racism reported in the media, such as ethnic violence or cases of racial discrimination. Even though you may have brought up your child to be tolerant, she needs to understand that people do have bigoted ideas and she will need courage to counter them.

GUIDELINES FOR YOUR ANSWERS

- Always try to put the point of view of people who are different because of appearance or custom. Encourage your child to accept all differences as normal variations, not as signs of inferiority or superiority.

- Explain that people who are racist are wrong and behave so because they're frightened or ignorant. Explain that any form of discrimination must be opposed and that you will support your child if she can stand up for fairness and justice whenever possible, as long as she doesn't put herself in danger.

WHAT ELSE TO KNOW

- When trying to explain racism and prejudice ask for your child's views. More often than not you'll find that your child is naturally fair and kind.
- Don't ever encourage prejudice in your child by running down or making fun of other groups on grounds of race, religion, dress, or colour of skin. If you have prejudices, spare your child. She is naturally impervious to suggestions of superiority or inferiority, so don't encourage such ideas in word or action.
- Children under six are only interested in gender differences, other differences don't bother them.

Other things you may be asked...

- *Why do people hate someone who looks different?*
- *Why do they call Akasi bad names?*
- *What should I do if they call me bad names?*
- *Why does Sabiha wear different clothes from us?*

See also *What is religion? p. 46* • *Why can't she walk? p. 70* • *What's a bully? p. 82*

A People who come from different countries in the world often look unlike each other, just as birds differ in appearance. But we're all people, no matter what we look like.

A People from different parts of the world often wear different kinds of clothes. In some parts of the world it's very cold and in others it's steamy hot and people who live there get used to wearing clothes that suit the place they live. Even when they move away, they like to go on wearing the things they're used to.

A Some people are frightened of others who don't look or talk the same. When people are frightened they sometimes think things which aren't true. We're all human beings who came from the same beginnings, even though people from Asia, Africa and Europe look different from each other now. We should accept people for what they are, not for what they look like, or the different way they live. But some ignorant people try to get the better of others by ganging up on them, or trying to stop them from getting jobs or places to live. It's good to stick up for Akasi – if someone calls him names, tell them not to and then tell your teacher or me.

A When people are frightened they often become aggressive. To make themselves feel more important, they make fun of people who look different. They may even use violence to try and make some people seem inferior. But of course this isn't true; just because you win a fight doesn't make you better than the person you beat. Some people will even fight wars because they think other people are inferior and must be suppressed. This is NEVER right. No one has the right to injure anyone else, let alone kill them. Always suspect someone who thinks like that, and talk it over with us. If people start saying bad things about you, try not to react – walk away. They're doing it because they are ignorant. If you see other people being bullied because of what they look like, try to stop it unless you're likely to be harmed yourself. Always tell Dad or Mum and we'll try to sort it out. Some people think people with brown skin are better than those with pale skin, or the other way round, but this is wrong – everyone is equal and we all have the same rights.

Q Why can't she walk?

- *Why does he look funny?* • *Why can't he speak properly?*
- *Why is she in a wheelchair?* • *Why is she all twisted?*
- *Will she get better?* • *Will I always be like this?*

Young children recognize the differences between people, and will articulate this. But as with their comments about people from different ethnic backgrounds, it doesn't mean they are prejudiced or disgusted about disablement; they will only become so if you fail to answer their questions on disabled people factually and sympathetically.

WHAT'S BEHIND THIS QUESTION

Your child isn't uncomfortable about people with disabilities in the way that some adults are. Your child may stare because he is curious, unlike the adult response to disabled people which is often to look embarrassed or even repelled. Your child is really only interested in differences in relation to himself, how they came about, if they could happen to him and whether they are permanent. Equally, if your child is disabled, he is just as likely to ask questions about other people with different disabilities. You can be reassuring on all these counts. Always stress that disabled people have the same rights as everyone else; they just happen to have a disability which makes their life more inconvenient than that of able-bodied people. Make it clear what strength is required to overcome this.

GUIDELINES FOR YOUR ANSWERS

- Even if you feel embarrassment, try not to show it, and give honest answers. You can explain that many disabilities occur as a result of accidents to the unborn baby or while a baby is being born. This information is reassuring for an able-bodied child because he'll know he got through those vulnerable times unscathed.

- Most disabilities are permanent, but with proper education, understanding and the implementation of legislation for access to public places, all disabled people can be helped to reach their full potential. Adaptation to their homes and transport can also help.
- Encourage your child to ask disabled people if they need help and to give it if requested.

WHAT ELSE TO KNOW

- You and your children should always make full eye contact with disabled people while talking to them.
- You could help your child to develop caring and nurturing instincts by taking him to visit disabled children in hospital or helping to take disabled people on outings – to the cinema or theatre, for example.
- Where appropriate support is available, disabled children are increasingly present in neighbourhood schools. If your school has a policy of integration, count yourself lucky, whether you are parents of an able-bodied or disabled child. Take the advice of the teacher co-ordinating special educational needs in helping to answer your children's questions.
- It's important for your child to understand that physical defects do *not* signify a slow mind or low intelligence and, like everyone else, disabled people have feelings that must be respected.
- It is equally important to encourage understanding of people with learning disabilities. Explain to your child that these people may experience life from a different perspective, but that they are not inferior in any way.

Other things you may be asked...

- *Was she born like that?*
- *Why is it rude to stare?*
- *Is she the same as me inside?*
- *Should I help anyone with a white stick?*
- *Why can't Granny hear what I'm saying?*

See also *Where did I come from? p. 12* • *Why isn't my skin brown? p. 68* • *What's a bully? p. 82*

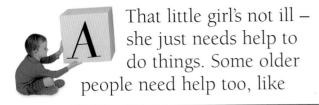

A That little girl's not ill – she just needs help to do things. Some older people need help too, like Granny. She's a bit deaf now so she can't hear you very well, but she's going to get a special hearing-aid to help her.

A People who are disabled can't always do all the things other people can, so sometimes people think you need help. They're only trying to be kind, so if they ask but you don't need help, just say politely, "No, thank you." You're very clever because you're learning to use special equipment which other children of your age don't have. We love you very much and you're very special.

A He's all twisted up because he probably couldn't breathe properly when he was being born and his brain didn't get enough oxygen. This sometimes stops his brain giving the right signals to his muscles. It's not his fault and sometimes it must be quite uncomfortable, but he will be learning to do lots of things on his own, even if he seems to be struggling at the moment, and he goes to school just like you do. People with disabilities aren't different from us inside, although they do need extra help and training to do everyday things that you and I might not have to think about.

A Disabled people are different from you in one of two ways – either they can't do some things the way you can, or they don't think quite the same way that you do. Most disabled people overcome their disabilities and lead happy lives – including getting married and having children. Just because a person looks or talks differently from you, or has to use a stick or a wheelchair, you must never make fun of them. Always remember that disabled people have the same rights as everyone else, and when you talk to a disabled person always look at them, don't turn away. But they also have the right to privacy, so people shouldn't keep snooping on them to make sure they're all right. And although able-bodied people have a responsibility to care for them, disabled people have the right to refuse help.

Q Do I have to eat meat?

- *Why do we eat meat?* • *Why do we make animals suffer for us?*
- *Do we have to eat animals to be healthy?*
- *Why do some people not eat meat?* • *What's a vegetarian?*

Your children may become aware of animal welfare issues surprisingly young, as popular films and television programmes for children focus on them more and more. It doesn't take them long to make the link between the lamb in the field and the roast in the oven; this could trigger resistance to meat-eating.

WHAT'S BEHIND THIS QUESTION

Children are much more sensitive about animal suffering than many adults because their sympathy for the pain animals might suffer at our hands is not tainted by adult justifications, such as "meat is good to eat", "animals aren't sentient beings as we are", "animals don't feel as we do", "animal skins have been used to keep human beings warm ever since man could hunt". Children focus solely on the possibility of pain and, in a very humane way, equate animals to people, believing them to have the same rights as us. It's an innocent approach and very clear and straightforward. It's also legitimate and should be taken seriously. It's not sentimental, it's about being fair and just to all living things.

GUIDELINES FOR YOUR ANSWERS

- You can't preach tolerance, kindness and compassion to your children and then expect them to accept cruelty in any form to animals. Try to welcome such a sense of fairness and to encourage it in them.
- Society's thinking is changing about animal welfare and animal rights are something everyone should think about and respect. Animals kept as pets deserve special treatment because they mean a great deal to their owners. Children learn about love for others through loving and caring for pets and no one would want to interfere with that. So respect your child's wishes if, as an owner of pets, she makes the connection between animals and food, and prefers not to eat meat.
- Be accommodating and accepting. Don't make fun of your child for caring about animals and not wanting to eat them. You'll be letting your child down if you do and she might not seek your help in future.

WHAT ELSE TO KNOW

- Very young children who refuse meat are unlikely to be doing it because they have realized it came from a live animal. At this age food preferences have far more to do with changing taste and experimentation. It may also come from a knowledge that mealtimes can provide an opportunity to assert their individuality.
- Be reassured that children can eat a fully vegetarian diet and be healthy, though they may need vitamin supplements, particularly from the B group, especially B12 which has no direct plant source.
- Support your child's decision to become a vegetarian by reading up as much as you can on it and making sure your child has a very wide diet of vegetarian foods.
- You have to eat very large quantities to obtain all essential nutrients from plant sources. If you are a vegetarian yourself, be alert to this; it may be difficult for a small child to accommodate the necessary bulk required to get enough nourishment. Think of your child before your vegetarian ethos.

Other things you may be asked...

- *Can children be vegetarians?*
- *Why do we kill animals to eat them?*
- *Do animals feel pain when they die?*
- *How do they kill animals for meat?*

See also What happens when you die? p. 40 • What is religion? p. 46

It's good for you to eat a little bit of meat and fish, because even a small piece has the goodness of lots of vegetables, and it's easier to eat! But we'll only have it once or twice a week and you can have cheese or eggs instead.

You don't have to eat red meat if you really don't want to but it would be good for you to eat some white meat, like fish or turkey or chicken. Yes, you can have your fish as fish fingers if you like. And I can make a special stew with soya, with lots of vegetables. The less meat you eat, the more vegetables and fruit you need to stay healthy, so try to eat as many kinds as possible.

A vegetarian is someone who doesn't eat any meat at all, even chicken, turkey and fish. People are vegetarians for many reasons. Some believe it is wrong to kill animals at all, and don't think it's right for animals to suffer just to feed humans, especially as animals sometimes live in very cramped conditions. Other people think growing crops just to feed animals that are killed for food is wrong when there are so many people in the world who haven't got enough to eat – they think the land should be used for crops to feed people instead.

Human beings are mostly "omnivorous", which means we eat animal and vegetable foodstuffs. Our bodies evolved to be able to use food from animal and vegetable sources. Humans have teeth to tear and chew meat, and chemicals called enzymes in our digestive systems to release the protein in meat, which is a very efficient food: small quantities contain lots of protein. But vegetarians need to eat lots more vegetables and fruit to get the same amount of protein.

We don't know for sure what happens to animals when they die, but we do know that all pain and suffering stops. The animals we eat are killed as painlessly as possible, but if you don't eat meat because you don't think animals should suffer at all, I will respect your wishes. Why don't you come with me to the supermarket so that you can choose which vegetarian foods you really like, then we can learn together how best to cook it.

QUESTIONS ABOUT

What's a bully?

Will all strangers hurt me?

Does AIDS hurt?

Why do people smoke?

Do I have to kiss him?

Why can't I talk to strangers?

Can I hit him back?

CHILD PROTECTION ● BULLYING ● VIOLENCE AND WAR ●

SAFETY & HEALTH

It is probably true that nowadays parents generally fear for the safety of their children in ways which may never have occurred to an older generation. While the world may be no more dangerous than it was, say, fifty years ago, parents are now increasingly aware of the dangers to which their children could be exposed. Knowledge of child abuse, both physical and sexual, is widespread; the damage to health of drugs, smoking and alcohol is widely publicized, and the spread of AIDS – a disease which by its very nature creates a climate of fear and uncertainty – is constantly reiterated by the media. It's not surprising that you may feel over-protective towards your young children, and wonder how to shield them from these constant dangers. Children need to believe that they can come to you about anything and that you'll take them seriously and believe them. You can help to build this trust by listening to their questions, believing what they say, and being ready to respond. Given enough accurate information to protect themselves, your children will grow up with a sense of proportion about all areas of personal safety and health.

Why did you shout at me?

Why do people get drunk?

SMOKING ● ALCOHOL ● DRUG ABUSE ● HIV AND AIDS

Q Why can't I talk to strangers?

- *Why mustn't I take a present from someone I don't know?*
- *Why can't I have a ride home in a stranger's car?*
- *Where can I go to get away from someone I don't know?*

Fear for the safety of your children is an unfortunate fact of modern life. However, it is possible to equip them with strategies to combat the unwelcome attentions of strangers. These will give you peace of mind, so that your children's movements don't have to be unnaturally restricted as they get older.

WHAT'S BEHIND THIS QUESTION

Children may be confused by the idea that what appears to be kindness from a stranger may be harmful. After all, you teach them that kindness is good, so they naturally interpret anyone's kindness in that way. In fact you have to warn your child about strangers before they're old enough to ask questions and you have to go on encouraging them not to trust people they don't know. Even when my sons were in their late teens I used to exhort them not to speak to strangers whenever they went into the city. To a child, anyone with sweets or toys on offer, or the promise of an exciting treat such as a visit to a fairground, is attractive, and someone who will save them a walk home is a godsend, so their questions will reflect their bewilderment at the contrary messages they seem to be getting about people's behaviour.

GUIDELINES FOR YOUR ANSWERS

- Because of children's innate trust of kind adults, they need to be taught one of life's tough lessons – that things may be more sinister than they seem. But it's important to strike a balance in what you say. You want to protect your children and give them enough information to protect themselves but you don't want them to lose their friendliness and become totally mistrusting of everyone. That would be unfair to your children, but their safety is paramount. It's not easy.

- The aim should be to educate your child in a non-alarmist way to steer clear of strangers whatever the inducements, so that it becomes part of normal life, a given, non-negotiable fact, like not touching electric power points or handling sharp knives.

WHAT ELSE TO KNOW

- Children need very clear instructions on how to act in certain circumstances. Draw up a checklist like a curbside drill and repeat it endlessly until your child knows it by heart. Make it easy to remember by including rhymes and rhythms. Make sure your child learns his address and telephone number – and his full name – as young as possible, and include the telephone number of a children's Helpline as well as your own.

- As a parent it is a good idea always to know where your child is. This may seem obvious but it is all too easy to be concentrating on something else and then turn round to find your child has wandered out of sight. At the same time you probably don't want to restrict an older child's movements completely. Make it clear from the start that the rule is that your child can go out if he is always with friends and that they all know the "drill" that you have been teaching your own child. Encourage your child to take responsibility for knowing exactly when he is expected home and always to telephone you if there is a change of plan.

- Encourage a bit of assertiveness so that your child won't be afraid to stand his ground. Play-act some possible situations with your child too, to make sure he is aware of what might happen.

Other things you may be asked...

- *Will all strangers hurt me?*
- *What do I do if someone talks to me?*
- *What do I do if someone gives me sweets?*
- *What do I do if someone offers me a ride in their car?*

See also *Why does his Mum shout at him? p. 80* • *What does violence mean? p. 84*

FOR AGES 2–4

A I don't like you speaking to people you don't know because they might not be kind to you. Even if they give you sweets, it could still mean they'd like to take you away. So never get into a car or go for a walk with anyone, even a child, without asking Mummy or Daddy first of all.

FOR AGES 4–6

A If you're lost and someone tries to talk to you, don't answer – keep away. Shout, stop the first woman you see, or go into a shop, and say "Please help me, I'm in danger." Then ask them to help you telephone us.

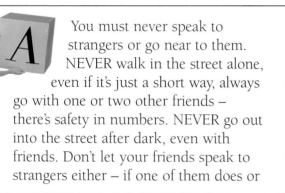

FOR AGES 6–8

A You must never speak to strangers or go near to them. NEVER walk in the street alone, even if it's just a short way, always go with one or two other friends – there's safety in numbers. NEVER go out into the street after dark, even with friends. Don't let your friends speak to strangers either – if one of them does or gets into a car, run straight home and tell us. If you're left alone, even if you know the way home, stay put and get someone to ring us and one of us will pick you up. If ever you're frightened or lost, ask a woman to help you and give her your name, address and phone number, or try to find a police officer.

FOR AGES 8–11

A There are people, mainly men, who like hurting children. You must try to stay away from them because they're stronger than you are. Being with a group of friends is a safeguard but if it's dark and you're taking a short cut home through the alley, then even a crowd of friends might not keep you safe. So always walk in wide, well-lit streets, at the outside edge of the pavement, stride out purposefully, keep your head up, swing your arms like a soldier and carry something like a sport's bag. Strangers hardly ever approach anyone walking like that. If a stranger ever gets hold of you, shout to your friends to get help quickly or to tell us or another grown-up they trust straightaway. Don't ever be rude to a stranger, and never pick a fight. If you get lost try and find a police officer or tell a woman in the street, or go into a shop, cafe or pub and ask if you can use the phone to contact us by reversing the charges. We'll give you a special phone card as well.

Q Do I have to let him kiss me?

- *Do I have to sit on his knee?* • *Is keeping secrets ever wrong?*
- *Is it ever right for someone to touch me down there?*
- *Are uncles/grandfathers always right?*

The possibility of sexual abuse of your child is something most parents prefer not to think about. But it does happen, and sadly the perpetrators are often people very close to the abused child – frequently in the same family. Abused children often feel doubly guilty if they reveal their abuse, so their questions may contain hidden clues.

WHAT'S BEHIND THIS QUESTION

The sort of questions I have given above are typical danger signs of sexual abuse, one of the most pernicious ways in which children can be exploited. Unfortunately it often involves someone close to the child, who can create an emotional smoke-screen based on "special secrets" combined with veiled threats. Many children are afraid of adults for quite innocuous reasons, but a child who is being abused often senses that something is really wrong, particularly if she is specifically being asked to keep something secret from her parents. Children who have been sworn to secrecy may be frightened to speak out, so be alert to questions that may signal that someone is taking advantage of your child's innocence. Be sensitive to other signs from your child, such as becoming withdrawn, refusing to eat, reluctance to visit a relative or having nightmares.

GUIDELINES FOR YOUR ANSWERS

- Children need to know that they can come to you about anything and you'll take them seriously. I get many letters from abused children who are scared to tell their parents in case they won't be believed.
- You need to be very calm and prepared for gentle probing to discover what has triggered the question. Make it clear that your child can tell you anything, even very big secrets, and reassure her that you'll protect her.

WHAT ELSE TO KNOW

- Most child sexual abuse is done by someone the child knows and trusts. This can be a shock, but you owe it to your child to believe her – avoid automatically dismissing what she tells you as fantasy or overreaction, or you may unwittingly perpetuate the abuse.
- Even when you point out that what the person has been doing is wrong, your child may feel she can't betray him, because she doesn't want him to suffer.
- All abused children think they're somehow to blame. Take time to assure your child that it's not her fault and that she won't get into any trouble if she's truthful.
- If it becomes clear that the abuser is the child's parent, then his partner must get help. The shame and grief this causes is terrible, but the prime responsibility must be to protect the child, not the abuser.

Other things you may be asked...

- *Do I have to sleep in the same room as him?*
- *Do I always have to do what a grown-up tells me?*
- *Do I have to obey older boys and girls?*
- *Will I go to prison if I tell someone's secret?*

See also What is sex? p. 18 • Why can't I talk to strangers? p. 76

A You never have to kiss or hug anyone if you don't want to. It's NEVER right for a person who's older than you to touch you down there, so you must always tell me. No, you don't have to keep secrets from Mummy, even if someone say something bad will happen if you do. Tell me at once and I'll make sure nothing bad happens to you.

A The only person you should always obey is Mummy. You should do as you're told at school in the classroom but not if a teacher wants you to do something alone with him which seems odd. You don't have to do anything involving touching or kissing that anyone else tells you to do. Just say, "I don't want to do that" or, "I don't want to play that game" or, "I want to go home now". If someone asks you to keep a secret about something, it usually means that they know Mummy would be cross if she found out, so it's wrong to ask you not to tell me. I can know all your secrets, especially if they make you unhappy. If someone tells you you'll go to prison or go to hell if you tell on them, they're wicked – it's a lie. They just say it to frighten you. Don't worry, Mummy can make things right and you'll never be blamed. No one will ever know you told me about them. You can always trust me.

A Some adults like doing sexual things to children, boys and girls. They're bad people and it's very wrong, because it's a particularly horrible kind of bullying. People like this think they can make you do things because they're stronger and older than you are and that is never right. It's against the law for anyone to do anything sexual to you against your will – that's what's called rape – and in most countries it's also against the law to have sex with anyone who's under the age of 16. If anyone tries to touch you in a sexy way, or wants you to touch them, even if it's someone in our family, tell them what I have told you. You don't ever have to do it, even if they offer you big treats. If you think that anyone is especially interested in you and might try to be sexual, tell Mum straight away and I'll make sure you're never with them on your own. Of course you don't have to share a bed when you go to your cousin's house. Just because he's older than you, you don't have to do what he says. I'll tell his parents you can't go there any more. Sometimes children think it's their fault if horrible things happen to them, but you must remember that it's never a child's fault if an older boy or girl or an adult tries to do something bad like this.

Q Why does his Mum shout at him?

- *Why do you have to shout at me?* ● *Is it ever right to hit someone?*
- *Why are you always cross with me?* ● *Why did you hit me?*
- *Why has Jamie got marks all over his legs and arms?*

Everyone has moments of stress, which may result in shouting at or smacking a child for a minor misdemeanour. Usually it passes, parents feel guilty, there are apologies all round and it doesn't happen again. But anything more than a light slap becomes abuse and everyone involved needs help.

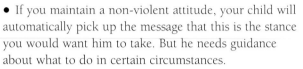

WHAT'S BEHIND THIS QUESTION

There are many kinds of abuse – even emotional abuse which may not show any physical scars – but most children believe that what happens to them is the norm, which is why even battered and abused children cling to their parents. Once a child's world widens beyond the home, he can make comparisons and may begin to realize that his situation isn't acceptable. Many children are afraid of adults who abuse them, and make excuses for their bruising: "I fell down", "I walked into a door". They may think, with some justification, that things will be worse for them if they reveal the abuse they are suffering. Another child, however, who sees the evidence of physical abuse, may speak out, especially if he sees a child being chastised for no apparent reason. A child whose teachers speak gently to him at school but who suffers verbal abuse at home will begin to wonder why there's a difference, even if he's used to being shouted at all the time.

GUIDELINES FOR YOUR ANSWERS

● Constant verbal abuse can brutalize children just as much as physical punishment and violence and no one sets out to bring up children in that way.

● If you maintain a non-violent attitude, your child will automatically pick up the message that this is the stance you would want him to take. But he needs guidance about what to do in certain circumstances.
● If your child asks you why you are being constantly aggressive or hurtful, take it seriously, and look at yourself critically. You will need to be able to justify your behaviour to yourself as well.

WHAT ELSE TO KNOW

Shouting aggressively is as much a form of abuse as hitting. If you constantly shout at a child, he won't know how to respond to normal levels of conversation. Regularly running him down, laughing at him, threatening to withdraw your love, or previously promised treats, are all forms of emotional abuse and could have a permanent effect on his self-esteem, so try to maintain a balance.

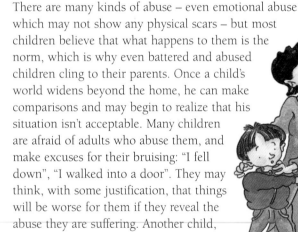

Other things you may be asked...

- *What's a battered baby?*
- *What do I do if a grown-up hits me?*
- *Should I tell someone if Jamie gets bruises again?*
- *Why are you always laughing at me?*

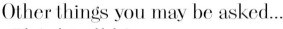

See also *Do I have to let him kiss me? p. 78* ● *What's a bully? p. 82* ● *What does violence mean? p. 84*

A This question is unlikely to be asked by children under four, although they may be frightened by receiving or even seeing, physical or verbal abuse. If a young child asks this question, base your answers on the 4–6 age band.

A I don't know why she shouts at him but whatever the reason it must make him sad. Perhaps her mother shouted at her and she thinks it's what all parents do. I sometimes lose my temper with you because I get cross too easily when I've got a lot to think about, but that's not an excuse. I love you very very much and I don't like shouting at you so I will try not to. Tell me if I start doing it again. If I ever hit you tell me the same thing because hitting is wrong too.

A People sometimes hit other people because they're angry or frightened. It's always wrong. No argument can be settled by a fight – it's best to try to talk it through. And if people won't talk, we should walk away. Jamie's got lots of bruises, hasn't he? A bruise shows where something has bumped hard against the skin. He might have got them falling over like he says, but if they're all over his body, there's probably another reason. If he comes into school with bruises again, tell me and I'll talk to the teacher. You'll probably help to stop Jamie from being hurt any more.

A I'm sorry if I hurt your feelings when I laughed at your drawings – I know you've worked very hard at them. Sometimes it's hard not to hit back, but if that boy hits you, tell him to stop and say if he hits you again, you'll hit him back. This will stop most people. But only hit him yourself if he hits you again and it's the only way to get away; then run and tell me or Dad or your teacher. We'll deal with it quietly, don't worry. But if an adult hits you – even if it's someone we know very well, you must tell me straightaway, and I'll sort it out. Some adults get angry inside when life is difficult and they take it out on children by hitting them, or not giving them enough to eat or things like that. A battered baby is one who has been hurt a lot by his parents. Often the parents love the baby really, but they can't cope with looking after it and treat it badly. It's never right. Sometimes the baby is taken away to be looked after by kind people while the parents get help so they can learn how to care for their baby properly.

Q What's a bully?

- *Why does David keeps hitting Andrew?* • *What's bullying?*
- *Why does he take my dinner money?* • *Can I hit him back?*
- *Will you stop those kids from picking on me?*

Bullying is one of the most insidious problems within schools – and it can exist in any school, no matter what the system or age of the children. Vigilant teachers in a school with a positive policy on bullying will be keen to nip it in the bud, so if your child's questions hint at bullying, take it to your school's headteacher immediately.

WHAT'S BEHIND THIS QUESTION

Questions about bullying are usually asked because your child has seen it at school or depicted on TV, but be on the lookout for signs of it happening to your own child. Sometimes you may have to be something of a sleuth. We only discovered one of our sons was being bullied because he kept asking us for more money – a gang of bullies at school were threatening to beat him up if he didn't give them money. Most children have a natural sense of fair play and hate to see classmates victimized, so they could question you about that too.

GUIDELINES FOR YOUR ANSWERS

- Bullying is always wrong and must be stopped. Convince your child of this fact in whatever way you can. She will find it easier to tell you about bullying if she is clear about this basic belief.

- Boys are particularly conscious of the ridiculous code that they mustn't tell on bullies, even if they are the victims. Convince your children that this code is wrong and that they must seek help if bullied.
- You may wonder whether your child should retaliate if faced with bullying. Under the age of nine, I used to tell my son to give the bully one warning and then hit back; but a child shouldn't do this if faced with several others. A child can ask a trusted older child to help deal with bullies, but you should always report bullying to the school, even if it is happening outside the school premises, and ask for the staff's help to bring bullies to book, in a discreet way to protect your child.
- Girls are just as capable of bullying as boys, and very often it takes the form of a cruel whispering campaign, or deliberately excluding a child from a group of friends. If prolonged, this can be just as wounding as physical violence, and should be taken seriously.

WHAT ELSE TO KNOW

- Children aren't born bullies but they often learn a pattern of selfishness, victimization and bullying from adults in their own homes. This may be due to excessive strictness from an authoritarian parent or arise in a home which is disorganized, where a child is neglected.
- Bullying is a child's response to pain, discomfort and lack of love, and can be one of a number of general behavioural disorders such as stealing, lying and truancy. While bullying can never be condoned, these children need help to change their pattern of behaviour.

Other things you may be asked...

- *Why does that girl keep smacking me?*
- *Why do people bully?*
- *What can I do if someone picks on me?*
- *Will he hit me if I tell the teacher?*
- *How can I stop them hitting him?*

See also *Why can't I make friends? p. 62* • *Why do I have to go to school? p. 64*

A If Nicky hurts you again, tell me and and I'll speak to the teacher for you. Lots of people are called names; I used to be called Dumbo because I was a bit plump – but it's just silly, so take no notice.

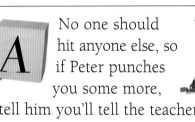

A No one should hit anyone else, so if Peter punches you some more, tell him you'll tell the teacher. You must tell the teacher and me, because Peter could hurt a lot of other people too. He's hitting people because he's very unhappy about something so he feels scared and lashes out. If we tell your teacher maybe we can all help him feel better about things.

A You know Mummy and Daddy don't approve of violence – punching and hitting – but bullies are wrong, they must be stopped. So this is what you do next time: give the bully one warning and say that if he attacks you again you'll hit him back, then go and tell your teacher what happened. Tell me, too, as soon as possible. And if he does hit you again, give him one big swipe, and then quickly go and tell your teacher. Don't try to hit back if there's more than one bully. Don't worry, your teacher knows how to deal with bullies, so I promise nothing bad will happen if you tell.

A Bullying is always wrong and bullies mustn't be allowed to get away with it. Picking on someone for any reason is never right. But that girl who is picking on you is probably very unhappy underneath, for some reason. Bullying is a way of pretending she isn't unhappy. But we have to think of how to stop her and then maybe someone will be able to find out why she's doing it. It isn't a good idea to try to hit back more than once – this will just lead to a fight, which bullies like. The best thing is to tell your teacher about it – ask a friend to come with you for moral support. If you have an older friend, I'm sure she'll help if you tell her about it. But do tell me because I won't let bullies victimize you. I'll go to the school and we'll work out with the teachers how to stop these bullies in a very discreet way.

Q What does violence mean?

- *Why are people violent?* • *Are football hooligans violent?*
- *Why do people blow things up with bombs?* • *What's a mugger?*
- *When people throw bricks through windows is that violent?*

Children are exposed to many violent images nowadays, and learn about violent situations from news bulletins and newspapers, so their reactions and questions may be confused. Striking a balance between your own desire to protect your children and keep them out of trouble, and the realities of war and terrorism, is very difficult for parents.

WHAT'S BEHIND THIS QUESTION

Over the age of four, children are old enough to know that violence – mental or physical – is undesirable, even wicked, and out of a sense of fairness will want some guidelines about how to recognize it, and how to act when they meet it. Out of a sense of injustice they may want to intervene precipitately but, as with bullying (p. 82), you'll have to coach them about when that's proper or safe and when to hang back even though their instincts are laudable. Children are also disturbed and confused by street and terrorist violence, and by the destructive images of war, which they see every day in newspapers and on television (fictional as well as factual) and whose causes are inexplicable to them.

GUIDELINES FOR YOUR ANSWERS

- To answer questions about violence sincerely you'll have to believe that violence is never justifiable, with the possible exception of some wars – though your children won't be able to understand this until they're eight or nine. Up to that age you won't go wrong if you condemn violence in all its guises as a most inappropriate way to solve problems or behave at any time.

- Violent adults breed violent children; we shouldn't pass on that legacy to a new young generation.
- Of course, for your children's own safety you will have to teach them that intervention in street violence is dangerous to them and they must avoid it.

WHAT ELSE TO KNOW

Your child is bound to meet violence sooner or later. I decided that much as I hated violence I could not go on forever teaching pacifism to my children, when they could come to serious harm if they thought they could rely solely on the intelligence of others to resolve arguments peaceably. So I taught them the "retaliate once and run" technique so that they would feel they had some control in unpleasant circumstances.

If you let your children watch TV on their own,
be aware that violent images can appear at any time.

Other things you may be asked...

- *Is being angry/cross/bad-tempered being violent?*
- *Is violence ever right?*
- *Is what happened in Ireland violent?*
- *When people go on a march, is that violent?*
- *What do I do if I see someone hurting my friends?*

See also *Why isn't my skin brown? p. 68* • *Why does his Mum shout at him? p. 80* • *What's a bully? p. 82*

Children under four are not likely to ask this question, although they are likely to see and be alarmed by violent behaviour. If a mature three-and-a-half year-old asks about violence, base your answers on those given for the 4–6 age band.

A Violence means really hurting or injuring someone because you don't agree with them or don't like them. You feel so angry you want to lash out and try to make them feel pain. It's never right. We can be cross with someone but that doesn't ever give us the right to hurt them. In some places, people plant bombs because they hate one another so much. Killing is the worst kind of violence and if they're caught, killers go to prison, sometimes for the rest of their lives.

A There are people who want to make others feel inferior by using violence to punish them. If you see someone being violent, don't get involved yourself, but get an adult to intervene. Sometimes people think violence is the only way of getting their own back for violence they have suffered themselves. That's why some people let off bombs – they think it's the only way they can get what they want. Regardless of their reasons, it's never right to be violent. When whole countries or different peoples in the same country are aggressive to each other it can lead to wars. Politicians try to stop wars by getting together to find ways of solving the basic problem.

A People of different races or religions sometimes hate each other enough to hurt each other or frighten people in their homes. If one group of people does that to another group with different skin colour or from another country, it's racial violence. This is always wrong as everyone has the right to live peacefully together, regardless of race, religion or nationality. Sometimes if people who have different views get together, for instance at a football match or a street demonstration, they get angry and start fighting and they might damage buildings and shops too. But it's never right to use violence to force your point of view. A mugger is someone who robs someone else in the street. If you see someone being mugged, don't intervene, you're too young, but hurry to tell an adult to get the police.

Q What's alcohol?

- *Why is alcohol bad?* ● *Why can't I have beer/wine?*
- *What does "drunk" mean?* ● *Why do you have wine at meals?*
- *What do I do if someone tries to make me have a drink?*

Alcohol is a drug, yet it is perfectly legal, so it is no wonder that children may be bewildered by the subject. There's plenty of publicity about the dangers of drinking and driving, and older children may be exposed to scenes involving drunks on television, so questions are sure to arise. You may need to think carefully about your own attitude towards drinking alcohol and how consistent you are.

WHAT'S BEHIND THIS QUESTION

For young children, the appeal of alcoholic drinks is a bit of a mystery, because they generally find the taste unpleasant. Older children asking questions like these are trying to work out why some things are all right for adults but not for them. It looks to them like a double standard and they are right, so you've got to have your thoughts very clear and your answers well worked out. Your child may also know someone who is suffering as a result of another's drinking, so you need to be alert and be prepared to provide discreet help.

GUIDELINES FOR YOUR ANSWERS

- Alcohol is a poison, but it isn't illegal, and it is difficult to convince children of this when they see so many adults drinking. But it is worth noting that anyone could die of alcoholic poisoning if too much is consumed too quickly – for instance, half a bottle of whisky in a couple of hours.
- The aim is to encourage your child to be sensible and moderate, and to take on personal responsibility for sobriety when she is old enough to drink alcohol.
- Most parents are aware of worsening statistics on underage drinking and so may be tempted to be strict;

I don't think this works. An authoritarian approach has negative results on almost all questions of discipline.
- By the time your child is eight or nine you can give her basic information on the harmful effects of alcohol. Children of this age are very receptive to arguments relating to good health and they'll usually respond well to calm and reasoned explanations.

WHAT ELSE TO KNOW

- I belong to the school of thought that believes anything that is banned automatically becomes very attractive to children. So sweets weren't banned in our house, nor was television, and nor was alcohol, but they were all rationed.
- Even very young children may like the taste of some alcoholic drinks but that's not a reason for giving it to them. Be aware that the new alcoholic "soft drinks" taste pleasant but are very strong. Avoid them. However, if adults are drinking wine with a meal I would give any child a taste who requested it. Up to the age of 10 most children dislike it and spit it out. After that some may enjoy wine diluted with a lot of water, and by about 12 or 13 like half a glass of wine neat.
- Help them to learn by your example; a good habit to instil in them from the start is never to drink alcohol on an empty stomach, but only at meal times with other people, and to have lots of water with it.
- Alcohol in small quantities taken with food is not unhealthy; some researchers believe that it actually confers extra years of life, so keep this long-term view in mind while teaching moderation.

Other things you may be asked...

- *How can you tell when someone is drunk?*
- *How do people get drunk?*
- *Which drinks are strongest?*
- *Why can't you drink and drive?*

See also *Why is smoking bad for you? p. 88* ● *What are drugs? p. 90*

Children under four are very unlikely to ask questions on this subject. However they may be curious if you are drinking alcohol, and questions may arise from that. If a young child asks a question, adapt my answer for the 4–6 age band.

A Alcohol is a chemical that is in drinks like wine and beer, and whisky and gin, which are much stronger. When people drink, it makes them feel relaxed, but it is a poison, so if people drink too much it makes them drunk, and they get out of control and feel sick and get a headache. But a little wine or beer isn't bad for most grown-ups at mealtimes.

A If people drink a lot of alcohol, they can become addicted to it, just like drugs or cigarettes. Drinking too much alcohol is very bad because it poisons the liver, and if the liver is worn out you die. Drinking alcohol also means you can't drive safely, even though people sometimes think they can, and people who drive when they're drunk often cause car accidents. No, I've never been drunk like that. We have wine with dinner because it's much safer to drink alcohol with food and it's relaxing when you're at home.

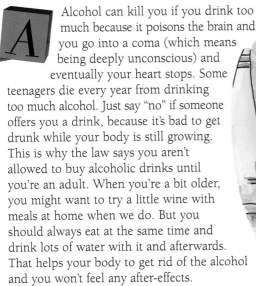

A Alcohol can kill you if you drink too much because it poisons the brain and you go into a coma (which means being deeply unconscious) and eventually your heart stops. Some teenagers die every year from drinking too much alcohol. Just say "no" if someone offers you a drink, because it's bad to get drunk while your body is still growing. This is why the law says you aren't allowed to buy alcoholic drinks until you're an adult. When you're a bit older, you might want to try a little wine with meals at home when we do. But you should always eat at the same time and drink lots of water with it and afterwards. That helps your body to get rid of the alcohol and you won't feel any after-effects.

Q Why is smoking bad for you?

- *Why do people smoke?* ● *Why do you smoke?*
- *Why does Grandpa smoke a pipe?* ● *What does smoking feel like?*
- *Why don't you give up smoking?*

Although fewer people smoke regularly nowadays, and smoking is forbidden in many public places, children are still regularly in contact with people who smoke, and the rate of teenage smoking is rising. Yet children are taught early on that tobacco is a legal drug which is bad for you, so they are bound to ask questions about it, especially if one or other of their parents smokes.

WHAT'S BEHIND THIS QUESTION

The anti-smoking lobby is very well-organized and your child will receive the message that smoking is bad for your health from quite an early age. He will also notice that in spite of this, people still smoke. If a family member smokes as well, your child will soon make known his puzzlement at the conflicting signals.

GUIDELINES FOR YOUR ANSWERS

- Even if you are a smoker yourself, you owe it to your child to point out the dangers of smoking to health, both to yourself and to others who inhale your smoke as "passive smokers".
- You need to try and put across the message forcefully that, unlike drinking alcohol, it is better never to start smoking, however strong the pressure may be from your children's friends. Stress how difficult it is to give up once you become addicted.
- Children up to 10 are less likely to be pushed into smoking, although some do, but it is a good idea to prepare them for the heavy peer group pressure that will undoubtedly surface in their early teens, when statistics show that cigarette smoking is unfortunately on the increase, particularly among girls.

WHAT ELSE TO KNOW

- Like alcohol, cigarettes are addictive drugs, but they happen to be legal. In some countries, however, it is illegal for anyone to sell cigarettes to children under 16.

● Your child may hear people say they shouldn't be prevented from smoking in public places like trains or restaurants. Counter this with the argument that underpins other public safety laws, such as speed limits on roads: that rights also involve responsibilities, and individual rights are over-ridden by the rights of everyone to safety and good health.

● If you're a smoker, you must be honest about why you smoke: even though you know it's bad for you, you feel it helps you relax and to concentrate better.

● A 1989 survey of 10,000 nine to 15-year-olds found that parental attitudes are important: children are less likely to smoke if parents are anti-smoking.

● A 1993 survey of 11 to 16-year-olds found that 85 per cent of boys and 83 per cent of girls aged 11 said they would never smoke.

Other things you may be asked...

- ■ *What do I do if someone tries to make me smoke a cigarette?*
- ■ *Why do so many people smoke if they know it's bad?*
- ■ *Why can't I buy cigarettes?*
- ■ *Why did Auntie Jean start smoking again?*

See also *What happens when you die? p. 40* ● *Why do some babies die? p. 42* ● *What's alcohol? p. 86*

Children under the age of four will rarely ask questions about smoking but may be curious if they see someone smoking.

If a mature three-and-a-half year-old raises the subject, base your answers on those I have given for the 4–6 age group.

A Smoking is always bad for you. It damages your heart and lungs and it also hurts people around you. Smokers find it difficult to give up, so it's best never to start at all.

A When people smoke, tar from the smoke gets inside their lungs and makes it difficult for them to breathe properly. This can take a long time, so some smokers think it will never happen to them. But we know that smoking causes lung cancer and heart attacks and lots of people die because of those two things. I used to smoke but I don't now. I stopped when you were in my tummy because smoking is bad for babies and children.

A Smoking is never good for anyone. It damages the lungs so that they get clogged up and it causes lung diseases, including cancer, which kill thousands of people every year. It also causes heart attacks because smoking makes people's veins and arteries tighten up and every year it also causes thousands of deaths from heart disease. Because it's so bad for you, it's against the law in most countries for children under 16 to buy cigarettes. The best thing is never to start smoking because it's addictive. This means your body gets used to nicotine, the drug which is in tobacco; it makes you want it all the time, so it's difficult to stop. But people smoke because they claim that it makes them less tense and helps them to concentrate. Luckily some people do manage to give up because they know it's so bad for them. And it's just as bad if you breathe in the smoke from someone else's cigarette – that's called "passive smoking". Young people start smoking because they think it's grown up but it isn't healthy. It's never grown-up or "cool" to make yourself ill. If friends offers you a cigarette, just say, "No thanks", and walk away. If they tease you, just say they're the ones who are silly because they're going to make themselves very ill. Remember that smoking makes their breath and clothes smell horrible and it will stain their teeth and fingers yellow.

● *What are drugs? p. 90*

Q What are drugs?

- *What happens if you sniff glue?* • *What's dope?*
- *Why do people die from taking ecstasy?* • *What's shooting up?*
- *What's crack-cocaine?* • *How do I say no to drugs?*

All parents worry about whether their child will experiment with drugs, although few consider that this might be relevant to the under-tens. However, drugs may now be an issue even for this age group, so if your child asks questions about drugs, it is far better to answer them accurately and straightforwardly than to duck the issue, so that she will be prepared for the future.

WHAT'S BEHIND THIS QUESTION

Whether we like it or not, drugs are now part of school culture. Taking drugs is seen by most young people as exciting and glamorous. It's also the subject of forceful peer pressure. Although children aren't generally exposed to drug-taking until they are at least 12 or 13, there is evidence that children as young as nine or 10 are dealing and taking drugs. While this is still fairly rare, your child could be exposed to drug talk quite early, so with questions like these, your child may simply be looking for information, but equally she may be asking for help. Be proud of your child for asking, try to ascertain how prevalent drugs are at school and report back discreetly to the headteacher.

GUIDELINES FOR YOUR ANSWERS

- You should try to prepare your child for exposure to drugs by giving specific advice on what to do and say to resist them. If possible, give this advice early enough to avoid her being caught unawares.
- What you say to your child should be honest but low key, in order to give her an accurate picture of the dangers of drug-taking, without being alarmist.

- The greatest antidote to taking hard drugs is high self-esteem, so make sure you help your child feel that she is great, and that you love her, come what may.

WHAT ELSE TO KNOW

- Marijuana is not addictive. On its own it probably does less harm than cigarettes, although many people smoke it with tobacco and there is evidence that heavy consumption can lead to memory loss. Smoking marijuana doesn't necessarily lead to hard drugs, so getting very upset about it is inappropriate. However, there is no getting away from the fact that it is illegal.
- Certain conditions make a child vulnerable to hard drugs: low self-esteem, being ignored, starved of affection, over-zealous discipline, a disorganized home with drunken parents.
- The newer drugs of the dance culture, such as ecstasy, are dangerous because their effect is unpredictable. You may convince your 10-year-old they can lead to death, but sustaining that fear on into her teens when she's exposed to them regularly will need careful handling.
- Sniffing solvents can be a problem even with quite young children. You should suspect solvent abuse if you find glue, lighter fuel or correcting fluid among your children's belongings, or if your child smells of the fluid. Solvent abuse can cause sudden death, so if you think your child has been sniffing solvents, call the doctor before you do anything else.
- Make sure your own consumption of alcohol or prescription drugs doesn't give your child an example of double standards to use against you in the future.

Other things you may be asked...

- *Is dope bad for you?*
- *Can you die from taking LSD?*
- *What does addiction/hooked mean?*
- *How do you die from taking heroin?*

See also *What happens when you die? p. 40* • *Why is smoking bad for you? p. 88* • *What is AIDS? p. 92*

Children under six are unlikely to ask questions about drugs or drug-taking unless they hear someone else mention the subject. If a mature child between four and six years asks about drugs, adapt my answer for the 6–8 age band according to your child's level of understanding.

A Drugs are chemicals that affect your brain. Hard drugs are cocaine and heroin, and crack – which is smokable cocaine. These are habit forming – you become addicted or hooked on them, which means you need to take them often and it's very difficult to stop. You don't want to eat and you become very thin and ill. Hard drugs can eventually kill you because they're poisonous and they can make you go into a coma and stop breathing. Soft drugs like ecstasy, marijuana, LSD and "magic mushrooms" are not addictive, but apart from marijuana, they can be very dangerous because they affect people in different ways. No one knows in advance how they're going to react. Even the first tablet could kill or make you so ill you never recover. It's best never to try them. Children have died the first time they've sniffed glue or other things like cleaning fluid. This is because they all have another chemical in them that affects the brain and makes you do and think stupid things. Sometimes these drugs can be like a terrible nightmare that never goes away – it's called a bad trip and some people never recover from it.

A "Dope" is marijuana. There are lots of other names for it like "pot" and "puff", "grass", "hash", "weed", "wacky baccy". Marijuana is usually smoked like a cigarette. People who smoke it now and then don't usually go on to hard drugs. It doesn't do you much harm unless you smoke it regularly, but it can damage lungs because people tend to inhale it more deeply than cigarettes, and it can affect your memory. People smoke marijuana because it makes them feel happy, but it is against the law. When you're older and start going to clubs, you might get offered pills like ecstasy. These are dangerous because you don't know how badly they will affect you. The best thing is just to say "No thanks", and walk away so the person trying to make you take one can't keep on at you about it. Tell him you don't need that kind of help to have a good time. People take hard drugs because they feel unhappy, depressed or lonely, or think that nobody loves them. But you know that we think you're terrific, and you should always think that too.

Q What is AIDS?

- *What's HIV?* ● *How do you get AIDS?* ● *Can anyone get AIDS?*
- *Does AIDS make you very ill?* ● *Does AIDS hurt?*
- *Do children get AIDS?* ● *Do all people with AIDS die?*

Information about HIV and AIDS must be an integral part of sex education for all children. Times have changed immeasurably from when the only reason for "safe sex" was to avoid unwanted pregnancies, so it is literally a matter of life and death to provide accurate and honest answers about AIDS, however distressing it may be.

WHAT'S BEHIND THIS QUESTION

AIDS is nearly always talked about in hushed whispers, so your child will probably know already that AIDS is something terrible and may be scared. He wants both truth and reassurance. Children may also be confused about the difference and relationship between HIV and AIDS, which are frequently confused by adults as well.

GUIDELINES FOR YOUR ANSWERS

- Try not to be homophobic. Don't blame it all on gays or bi-sexual people, or let your child believe that only gay men get AIDS. Many newly reported HIV positive cases are from heterosexual contacts, though most HIV positive people in the USA, Europe and Australia are homosexual men. In Africa and Asia, AIDS is mainly a heterosexual problem.
- You will have to explain the difference between being HIV positive and having full-blown AIDS, know something about how the virus behaves, how it can be treated and how it causes death. This background information will help, but it is much better for you to do a bit of homework to become better informed.
- Although HIV is a virus, it is not contagious like the common cold or 'flu. It's quite hard to catch HIV – only a "pathological" dose, found in semen, blood and possibly vaginal fluid, will infect a person.
- Emphasize the need for safe sex – wearing a condom every time you have sex; a woman's right to insist that a man wears a condom; or no sex at all. Sow the seeds of sexual responsibility.

- Explain to your child that AIDS itself is extremely serious, but make it clear that there is no need to avoid normal contact with people who are HIV positive.

WHAT ELSE TO KNOW

- AIDS stands for Acquired Immune Deficiency Syndrome; HIV stands for Human Immunodeficiency Virus. Once a person has sufficient viruses in the body, antibodies are produced and these can be picked up on testing. If the test is "positive" for antibodies, the person is said to be "HIV positive".
- Most researchers believe that infection with HIV leads to the eventual breakdown of the body's immune system, leading to AIDS. This means the body is unable to defend itself against infections, leading eventually to death. There is no reliable treatment for AIDS.

Women nearly always contract HIV from sexual intercourse with infected men.

Other things you may be asked...

- ■ *Can you get AIDS from kissing?*
- ■ *Can you get AIDS from shaking hands?*
- ■ *Can you tell when someone's got AIDS?*
- ■ *Can you get AIDS from going to the toilet?*

See also *What is sex? p. 18* ● *What does it mean if you're "gay"? p. 36* ● *What happens when you die? p. 40*

Children under six are unlikely to ask this question because they probably won't come across the term at this age. If the subject comes up, say: "AIDS is a serious illness that can kill people. You won't die of it – you won't even get it. You won't die till you're very old."

FOR AGES 2–6

A AIDS is a very serious disease. It's caused by a virus called HIV, which stands for Human Immunodeficiency Virus. When someone catches the virus the person can have a blood test done which comes up "positive", so the person is called "HIV positive". The virus is mostly in people's blood, or their sperm if they're men, so it is quite difficult to catch it – mostly people only catch it now if sperm with the virus in it gets into their bodies, if they're drug addicts using needles or they had a bad blood transfusion. But in most countries you can't get it from blood transfusions any more because all blood is tested to make sure it's safe. Anyone could catch HIV, but most people don't because they are very careful. Very few children get AIDS; it happens if a woman was HIV positive while a baby was growing in her tummy. Very few children outside Africa or Asia die of AIDS. When people get the virus, at first they haven't got proper AIDS, but so far every grown-up who's HIV positive gets AIDS eventually, even though it may take years. But while someone is HIV positive he may not be ill at all, and can get on with normal life.

FOR AGES 6–8

A HIV can only infect you from blood or semen. You can't get infected with HIV from going to the toilet, or swimming, or shaking hands, or from kissing or drinking from the same cup, so you can kiss and hug people with HIV or AIDS. In fact people with AIDS need lots of love and kindness because they are very ill and will die as a result of having the virus. HIV damages the body's immune system – the way it fights diseases. If the immune system does not work, the body gives in to any germs that come along. AIDS is really the name for the whole list of symptoms and diseases a person with HIV eventually gets. HIV is normally passed on during sex because there are more viruses in semen than anything else. Men can pass it on to women or other men. Lesbians who have never had sex with a man don't usually get AIDS. But HIV also gets passed between drug users who share needles to inject themselves. When two people have sex, the man should always wear a condom; if he is HIV positive the virus can't be passed to his partner in semen. This is part of "safer sex", which means having sex in a way that stops HIV from being passed on.

FOR AGES 8–11

INDEX

Acknowledgments

Dorling Kindersley would like to thank:

Annette O'Sullivan for design assistance; Sarah Ashun for assisting the photographer; Wendy Holmes for make-up; Daisy Hayden for research; Elaine Harries for editorial assistance; Hilary Bird for the index

and the following children for modelling:

Ellie Blancke (2), Chrystell Brett (7), Stephanie Brett (4), Cassie Clarke (10), Daniel Clarke (7), William Duffus (8), Holly Durkin (5), Lauren Fernandez (4), Emily Gorton (6), Kashi Gorton (9), Shanti Gorton (4), Ethne Grey-Still (4) Thomas Greene (7), Thomas Holme (3), Megan Lacock (3), Claire Leonard (9), Lydia Leonard (9), Megan Leonard (6), Mitchell Leonard (3), Daniel Lord (4), Maija Marsh (7), Hayley Miles (2), Farid Mohamed (4), George Shellabear (4), Miriam Shellabear (2), Rebecca Shilling (10), Matthew Smith (10), Amy Walton (5), Calam West (9), Kera West (7).